The
HAYWAI

The Sergison Arms, Haywards Heath.

Wyn Ford

with the assistance of Lilian Rogers

𝕾.𝕭. 𝕻ublications

First published as *The Metropolis of Mid Sussex*, 1980
This edition published in 1998 by S.B. Publications,
c/o 19 Grove Road, Seaford, East Sussex BN25 1TP.

ISBN 1 85770 141 0

Printed by Island Press,
3 Cradle Hill Industrial Estate, Seaford, East Sussex BN25 3JE
Telephone: 01323 490222

Front Cover: Looking towards Commercial Square
Back Cover: Oaklands. At the time of the 1871 Census, the house
was occupied by Harry Treacher, a Brighton bookseller.

CONTENTS

PREFACE TO THE FIRST EDITION

HAYWARDS Heath 'must be the metropolis of Mid-Sussex'. That was the opinion expressed by representatives of St Wilfrid's church in December 1877. In support of this they made a number of observations. The population was increasing, and the town now catered for the majority of the poor of Cuckfield. The Primitive Methodists had recently opened a chapel in Sussex Road, and the Congregationalists had already been established in Wivelsfield Road in 1861; in both the staff of the Sussex County lunatic asylum had active members. Furthermore, the railway station saw 'upwards of seventy trains' each day. But the leisured elite did not show much concern for the place. 'The few rich residents also have houses in Brighton, plead double calls, and do not take the same interest as though St Wilfrid's was their actual home.'

Since its inception at the beginning of 1862 the growth of the town had been impressive, suggesting the release of pent up energy. St Wilfrid's church was built at the outset, in 1862-5; but it had been preceded both by the Congregational church, derived from a mission established in 1857 at Haywards Heath to cater for the workers at the asylum, and by the church school, which had been set up in 1856. Soon after the consecration of the church, the area was designated in 1866 a district chapelry, and was advanced to the status of a parish in 1872, with a board as constituted under the Local Government Act of 1858, although the population enumerated the previous year was under the lower limit for such a body prescribed under the amending Act of 1863. In 1880 the board changed its name from that of the church to the Haywards Heath Local Board; the previous year the Congregational church was registered for solemnizing marriages and the Strict Baptist chapel had been built by William Knight in the same road. The growing nonconformist element in the Sussex Road area suggests an increasing degree of social polarization between the leisured and professional classes on the one hand and tradespeople on the other, although the town's identity was recognized in 1870 by *Kelly's Post Office directory* in according it a separate entry. In 1879 the importance of the area was further demonstrated by the publication of *Clarke's local directory*.

The town naturally suffered from the depression of the 1880s. But its progress continued, and it achieved the status of a civil parish through the constitution of an urban district council in December, 1894.

What follows is an attempt to trace some of the features in the development of Haywards Heath from the earliest signs of human activity through its settlement as a number of scattered farms to its eventual urban condition. It is not the full story: that would take too long in the telling. Plenty of detail has been left out, and much more has eluded us. The detailed analysis of Census and other material that might be attempted has been left for other occasions and perhaps other hands. We hope that our story will lead to a fresh appreciation of the history in this place.

Many people have helped us in our researches, and to them all, both living and dead, we are deeply grateful. We would mention especially the local detail we have gained from the late Miss M Cartwright, Mr Frank Clarke, Mr George Edwards, Mr Claude Ferguson, the late Mr A G Maller and Miss M E M Walton. Mr F G Hilton, Messrs Thomas Bannister and Company and the Secretary of St Francis Hospital have allowed access to records in their keeping, and the staffs of the East Sussex Record Office, Brighton Central Reference Library and the Guildhall Library have borne with fortitude the demands made upon them. Mr N Caplan, Mr J B W Heyman, Mr Richard Moon and Mr C J Oxley have been kind enough to help with advice or criticism, although none of them is responsile for the errors that remain. Free access to the library of the *Mid Sussex Times* has supplemented personal resources and memories in compiling the later sections of the book, and this is greatly appreciated; and Mr Geoffrey Cohen has applied a gentle spur.

Finally, it should be mentioned that this is a joint, but not a co-operative, venture. Wyn Ford is responsible for the introduction, the four chapters in the first section, the appendix and the bibliography. He has not attempted to carry the story beyond 1900, although later details have been included. Conway Gabe has carried the account to the present day in the remaining sections.

WKF
ACG
September 1980

PREFACE TO THE REVISED EDITION

IN this revision of *The Metropolis of Mid Sussex* the first four chapters have been little altered apart from necessary amendments, but the latter part of the book has been entirely rewritten, and a fresh selection of illustrations has been made.

In the work of revision I have had the enthusiastic help of Lilian Rogers, who has spent almost all her life in Haywards Heath. She has shared with me her fund of knowledge of the town and its past, and without her help this revision would have been much the poorer. Many of the photographs come from her unique collection.

I have been helped also by, among others, Peggy Gould, Fred Fairhall, Harry Ellmer, Rebecca Kemp, Eileen Hollingdale, Pat Avery, John Lawrence, Brian Sargent, Shirley Bond and Steve Watts. Michael Denman, David Vaughan and Janice Brinley-Codd have helped with photographs, and the picture of Waugh and Company's old office is included with the permission of Jack Cookson. I am very grateful to them all. I am grateful also to the chief executive of the Mid Sussex District Council, Bill Hatton, for allowing me to use the records of his planning department, and to Carol Ratcliffe and her colleagues for their ready co-operation in producing them for me. I have also utilized material from the late Alfred Maller, a former teacher at what is now Oathall Community College.

Despite all the help I have received and my attempts to avoid them, errors are almost inevitable, and for them I must accept responsibility.

Wyn Ford
July 1998

THE AUTHOR

WYN Ford first moved to Sussex in 1956, and lived in Haywards Heath for nearly 31 years before moving to Keymer in 1996. He was educated at Wells Cathedral School, Epsom College and London University, and holds a Bachelor's degree from the Open University. During his lifetime he was a Fellow of the Royal Historical Society, an honorary member of the Sussex Archaeological Society, and Vice-Chairman of the Friends of the East Sussex Record Office. In addition to the books on Haywards Heath listed in the bibliography, he had published *Music in England before 1800: a select bibliography* (1967) and *Chichester diocesan surveys, 1676 and 1724* (1994).

Wyn Ford died in September 1998, shortly before this book was published.

BEGINNINGS

THE area in Kent and Sussex known as the Weald derives its name from the great wood that extended between the North and South Downs from the Kent coast around Folkestone as far as Petersfield in Hampshire. Some fifteen hundred years ago, we are told, Aelle and his companions drove the Britons into 'the wood which is called Andredsleah' after they had landed at Selsey. The hint that they were deterred by the density of the trees is supported by other evidence. When William the Conqueror came to found his abbey at Battle, the site was chosen for its remoteness, and the principal remains of earlier periods are clustered on the Downs.

Yet it would be quite wrong to regard the Weald as an impenetrable jungle uninhabited before modern times. There was an iron industry from Roman times, with workings in the West Hoathly-East Grinstead area. These were served by two roads passing across the Weald: the London-Brighton Way, which passed through Felbridge and close to a large cemetery at Hassocks that seems to have been used from the first century AD to Saxon times; and the London-Lewes Way, which went through Edenbridge, Isfield and Barcombe. Stane Street was another road crossing the Weald from London; it traced its way to Chichester through Slinfold, Billingshurst and Pulborough.

It is the first of these roads that interests us. Its path has been traced from the south as far as Bolnore, and from thence it probably skirted the former hospital grounds to the west, crossed Lucastes Avenue and proceeded northwards across the Penland-Harland estate to cross Balcombe Road just to the south east of the Penland Road junction to cross the railway at Sugworth Farm. This suggests that there was at least a transitory settlement in the area at this period. Much earlier evidence lies in the discovery of a Bronze Age pot in peat at Haywards Heath; later evidence of settlement in the area is provided by an Anglo-Saxon pagan burial at Hickstead Place, Twineham.

Early charters give us more definite information about permanent settlements. During the eighth century we hear of grants of pasture rights, woodland and swine pasture in the Kent Weald, and place name evidence shows that the same kind of thing was happening in the Sussex Weald also. Names associated with pigs and sheep or other animals occur, as do those associated with trees, such as Lindfield with the linden tree, frequently used as a meeting-place; or Wigperry (the name of land near Butlers Green), which means 'Wicga's pear tree'. Personal names like this, or Boltro ('Bollas's tree') or associated with the element -*ing* ('the people of') are characteristic of the area, as are those proclaiming some form of clearance.

As early as 770 there was a church at Henfield, 4 miles from Twineham, for we find record of a grant of land to it in that place. The charter of about the same date relating to an estate stretching from Stanmer to Lindfield and beyond is probably bogus, but it seems to delineate the kind of extensive estate that lay behind the silence of Domesday concerning the Weald. Even as late as 1086 it seems that the only iron working in Sussex was still in the East Grinstead area, and there were numerous settlements between Ifield and Worth, where there is an important pre-Conquest church, although Domesday indicates that almost no one lived there; and lying closer to what is now Haywards Heath there were settlements at Horsted Keynes, Sheffield Park and Fletching. We see that the name given to the group of estates into which the last three fell was Rushmonden, which includes the name *denne*, a word used for swine pastures in woodland separated from the manors to which they belonged.

This gives us a clue to understanding what Domesday has to say about the area of Haywards Heath. For in the group of estates that included it, as in the adjacent groups, all the settlements lay at the foot of the Downs. We take the information given for them as including also the lands belonging to them in the Weald. Most of the estates are shown as belonging to William de Wateville, a military tenant of the Earl of Warenne, who held lands at Brighton, Hangleton, Perching (in Fulking) and Barcombe as well, in addition to lands in Surrey; his position was unusual in that his wife also held land in the hundred of Buttinghill, as our group of estates was called. Further inland the land was held by a variety of tenants.

By the end of the century the landscape had changed appreciably from that suggested at the time of Domesday. We hear of churches at Ardingly, Balcombe and Wivelsfield (where it may have been built before the Conquest), as well as at Cuckfield and elsewhere in Mid Sussex; at Bolney the church itself is evidence that it was built by that time.

All this suggests increasing clearance and settlement in the Weald during the eleventh century, a process that we know continued in east Sussex estates during the next two centuries.

It is at this period that we first meet the name Hayworth, the earliest form of Haywards Heath. The earliest surviving records of the barony of Lewes show it as a personal name that implies the recognition of the place. There are several references in 1265-6 to Philip of Hayworth as acting as surety with John of Bolnore for William of Wigperry in an action for trespass, and there is also a

8

reference to Thomas of Hayworth in 1266. That at least two men bore the name shows clearly enough the settled nature of occupation in the area, and a reference to William's son Reginald suggests that other colonizations had occurred in the vicinity; another settlement is clearly indicated by the name John of Bolnore. A little earlier, in 1235-6, we come across Ralph of Sugworth answering a warrant from John, chaplain of Plumpton, to take rent from Thomas and Alice of Hurstpierpoint.

Later on, in 1290, we find Philip serving on a jury at West Hoathly inquiring into lands there held of the manor of Plumpton, together with men bearing the names Gravetye and Birchinestye (Burstye, north of Lindfield). In 1296 he served on another jury, this time in Brighton to inquire into lands at Streat, together with men from Sugworth, Gravelye and Chittingly, among others, and he also acted as assessor for the lay subsidy that year in the hundred of Streat (which included Lindfield), again with William of Chittingly, and William of Wigperry also reappears.

It seems that at this period the area lay in the hundred of Streat, and not with the parish of Cuckfield in the hundred of Buttinghill; but among those assessed in Cuckfield appear the name John of Heggeneswerth, and this name may be a variant of Hayworth. None of these names appear in the assessments for the next two subsidies in Cuckfield, however, although Thomas of Hayworth appears as assessor in 1327 for the vill of Lofield, which lay in the south of the hundred of Streat; but when John of Hayworth assigned some land in 1358, the deed described him as of the parish of Cuckfield, and one of the witnesses had been assessed for tax in that township in 1332; another was William of Bolnore and a third John of Stanford, a place we shall come across later.

The name Hayworth is taken to indicate some sort of fence or enclosure. We can be fairly definite about what kind of enclosure it was. We know that much of the Weald was afforested, that is, reserved for conserving game for the use of the king or local magnate (in this case the Earl of Warenne); there is a letter from Edward 1 addressed to the warden of the chace at Cuckfield and Worth, and in the enquiries of 1279 the jurors of Buttinghill hundred, in responding to a question about animal reserves, complained of the damage done to the crops by the animals of those who lived close to the unenclosed reserves. We know from Domesday that these reserves possessed special enclosures called *haiae* or hays, in which game was conserved for hunting. Thus the name Hayworth seems to mean an enclosure for keeping animals for sport.

When we come to discover where Hayworth was we are on firmer ground. The clue is given in the manorial map of 1638, the first detailed information that we have. Conspicuously marked on it is the land round Great Haywards Farm, extending from Haywards Road westwards to Isaacs Lane and including

Chownes Road, and bounded on the north by Muster Green and South Road, and on the south by Ashenground Road. We can be so definite on the matter because Great Haywards farmhouse has been dated about 1400, and the same date has been proposed for Little Haywards in Courtlands, which is referred to in the Cuckfield parish registers in 1607 as 'East Haiworth of Hardhams' (ie the land occupied by Nicholas Hardham of Great Haywards). As we shall see, Sussex Road is an old highway, so the enclosure could never have extended farther eastwards; and for the same reason Ashenground Road marks its southern limit. Its northern boundary was at Butlers Green Road. We can tell this because the words 'Trubwick waste' occur on the map just to the west of Butlers Green house. We have now to explain what Trubwick was.

We know that Trubwick (as distinct from Hayworth) was a manor held from Plumpton Boscage. This latter appears first in the early sixteenth century, and seems to have been one of the offshoots of the manor of Plumpton. If Boscage means 'woodland', as probably it does, then we may take it that Plumpton Boscage was a manor formed to organize the outlying woodland belonging to Plumpton. Even at the time of Domesday it was a sizeable manor, with lands in Falmer, and not unreasonably we may suppose that it possessed woodland some distance away in the Weald. In 1597 'the Buskage' included lands in Lindfield as well as Sharpthorne (near East Grinstead) and Tickeridge (West Hoathly). where there is an early fourteenth century hall. Probably Trubwick also was farmed out from the outset as a freehold tenement belonging to Plumpton, with a hall at Butlers Green, on the road from Cuckfield to Lewes. The first we hear of the place is in 1275-6, when Robert of Rogate, who already had a considerable estate at the village near Midhurst, gave to John of Trubwick and his wife Cecilia land, woodland and a house in Trubwick and Hayworth. John was the son of a twice widowed lady named Maud of Trubwick; and thereby hangs a tale.

For both Maud's father and her first husband, Walward of Wadhurst, owned property in Apuldram. It was presumably when she married again that she came to Cuckfield; but that is far from certain, since the surname 'of Trubwick' occurs at the end of the twelfth century at Boxgrove. Among those responsible for fencing Aldingbourne park in 1256-7 was Richard of Trubwick; but the list includes Henfield township and 'the men of Cowfold', so Richard may have been Maud's second husband living in Cuckfield. What is significant is the number of places in the vicinity of Chichester. John seems to have returned to the area within ten years of gaining the land at Cuckfield: the name is that of a witness to a charter in Sidlesham in about 1287, and occurs in the scutage assessment at Sidlesham at about the turn of the century. He seems to have died by 1296, because Cecilia alone was taxed in that year.

The name was absent that year from the Cuckfield returns. But it survived in Cuckfield as that of the manor immediately to the north of Butlers Green and to the west of Hayworth. It has now disappeared; but other local place names with medieval origins still survive. Franklyns Manor seems to have originated with the Dyrild Fraunkeleyn noticed in the 1332 tax assessment for the vill of Lofield; Hurstwood may derive its name from the Walter at Hurst mentioned in 1440; as we shall see, the name existed a century later. We can trace the history of Penlands Farm in a series of deeds starting in 1434, and other farms in the area probably have a medieval origin if the dating of surviving houses is any guide.

In the Middle Ages, therefore, the area of Haywards Heath had scattered over it a number of isolated farmsteads. It was crossed by roads leading from Cuckfield and London to Lewes. One route to London lay through Lindfield, where we know that some London men possessed land.

But it is in connection with a third parish, Wivelsfield, that we first hear of Haywards Heath itself. In 1504 William At Tree, lord of the manor of Otehall, conveyed to John Michelborn a piece of land called Brekespers lying next to Hurstwood, Hurstland and the King's highway leading from Syffordseresse (?Seaford) towards Haywyrddyshoth. Later in 1540 in a similar transaction we hear of land on the common of Haywords Hoth beside a copse called Hochfelds leading to the road from Cuckfield to Lewes; and in 1547 we are told of wasteland in the parish of Wivelsfield near Haywards Hoth owned by Thomas Godman south of the common land of the heath called Fellride, lying just to the east of South Road. In 1544 John Skrak (Scrase) had property beside the heath.

Thus we are getting a picture of settlement just to the south of the present town. In 1569 the waste called Haywards Heath, with the trees growing thereon, was claimed by the barony of Lewes. Only the manorial tenants of Trubwick were known to have any right to pasture their cattle there, and it was said that the lords of Trubwick only had felled trees there during the previous half century. Nevertheless, there is a mention of the manor of Hayworth as early as 1542; this seems to have been a small affair restricted to demesne farming in the Hayworth enclosure, with no rights on the heath.

We get a clearer view of the situation in the following century. To this we shall turn in the next chapter.

Great Haywards,
The Manor House,
dated *c*1400,
front elevation.

The rear elevation.

Little Haywards in
Courtlands, dated
*c*1400

1639 AND ALL THAT

We have already met with the map of the two manors that was compiled during the summer of 1638. Its title proclaims it to be a 'survae of the land belonging unto Nicholas Hardham'. Although the manors of Hayworth and Trubwick were combined by that date, it seems that they were distinct until the end of the previous century. In 1542 John Robardes bought Hayworth from Nicholas and Agatha Mascall, of Sherrington, near Lewes, who were interested in the parish of Wivelsfield. In 1546, however, Thomas Michell of Worth, who had been a commissioner of sewers in 1534 and ranger of Worth forest and whose landed interests spread over a wide area, made over Trubwick to Michael Homewood, a Cuckfield husbandman. The subsequent histories of these manors need not detain us, but it is interesting to notice that all the last three parties have surnames that appear in one of the Wivelsfield deeds noticed in the last chapter: the adjudicators in a dispute over lands in an area extending from Balcombe to Hurstpierpoint which had belonged to Walter Othale included John Michell of Cuckfield, the father of Thomas, John Homwood, who seems to have been in Cuckfield in 1486, and John Mascall, whose name appears with Thomas Michell's in a grant of the manor of Westmeston in 1541. This dispute occurred in 1502, and Nicholas Mascall was involved in another transaction concerning the manor of Otehall in 1534.

All this suggests a rather tenuous link at an early date between the two manors and the parish of Wivelsfield. It is interesting to notice in this context that a weaver named John Martin was described as 'of Haywarde' when his daughter was baptized at Cuckfield in 1604, yet he was a tenant of the manor of Keymer in 1613 as occupant of a 'parcel of Haywardes hothe'. He had acquired in 1595 land to the east of the heath, in the area designated 'Tenants lands' on the map; the holding included a house, barn, shop, an orchard and a hempyard. We should notice also that some 17 acres of the heath itself was held to belong to the manor of Keymer at this period.

In 1594 the manors came together under one lord when Thomas Jenner and James Hardham acquired Hayworth and a majority interest in Trubwick. Jenner was a Lindfield man who had lived in Cuckfield for 20 years; when he drew up his will in 1599 he appointed as his overseers a Lindfield tailor, Walter West, and a Cuckfield husbandman, Robert Johnson. He makes no mention of manors, although he refers to 'my freehold Lands . . . in the parrishe of Cuckfilde & Called by the severall names of Butlers, Stockland, little Haywards and Gubride'. Of James Hardham there is no mention; but the two witnesses to the will were Robert Johnson and Nicholas Hardham. Nicholas married Anne Jenner, probably one of the daughters remembered but not named in the will, and they had settled at Great Haywards by the time their third daughter was born in May 1605; Jenner had conveyed the tithes to Nicholas before he made his will. The family continued to live at Butlers Green and children were born there both to Thomas the younger and to his brother Stephen.

By 1613, however, another family had arrived at the house, for the parish register records the burial on 6 November of an unnamed infant son of John Warden 'of butlers green'. Possibly he had arrived from Findon, but was already described as of Cuckfield in the previous year when Thomas Jenner, who had then settled in Brighton, made over to him both the house and part of the manor of Trubwick. Thenceforth the Warden family lived in the house until the death of Francis Warden in 1785.

We do not know when Nicholas Hardham first appeared on the scene. An earlier Nicholas was a Brighton butcher who died in 1567. From his will it is clear that he had links with Chichester, and it is interesting that our Nicholas described himself as a yeoman of Tillington beside Petworth park, when he came to draw up his will just before his death at the end of 1626; although two of his brothers lived near him in Cuckfield, a third was a Tillington yeoman, and Nicholas himself bequeathed to Anne his wife the 'best bedsteed . . . in my house at Tillington' amongst other things. In 1609 he had been a churchwarden at Cuckfield, and 10 years later his name appears in the list of the seven 'occupiers' of the Haywards portion of tithes in 1619. But it seems that he spent his last years increasingly at Tillington; of the four overseers of his will, three came from the extreme west of the county: Lodsworth, near Midhurst; Hunston, near Chichester; and his Tillington brother, Thomas. The fourth was Jeffrey, his only surviving brother in Cuckfield, who plays a further part in our story.

To his second son, the Nicholas of the map, was bequeathed 'all that my Mannor called . . . Trubwicke . . . together with the Court Baron thereunto belonging, with all the rights . . . wastes, Commons', with his house and lands. Apart from the indication on the map of a court house on the site of Steeple Cottage, this mention of the domestic manorial court is the only trace of it that has survived from this period. There is no mention of Hayworth; probably this was implicit in the name of the house.

The younger Nicholas had been born at Great Haywards in 1610, and thus was a lad of 16 when his father died. It was therefore prescribed in the will that until he reached the age of 25 Jeffrey should rent the manor. Jeffrey was described as 'an honest man'; but unfortunately he survived for 3 years only, and presumably the affairs of the manor rested with the elder son John; he seems to have been self-willed, with his own affairs in Tillington.

This may have had some bearing on the subsequent course of events. Even in 1626 it seems that the manor was not free from debt, for the elder Nicholas prescribed that wood from the manorial lands should be sold to meet them. The younger Nicholas died at the beginning of 1662. In his will drawn up three months earlier, he allowed his executors to sell both Great Haywards and the manor to defray debts outstanding at his death: his wife Elizabeth was left with £200 and 'the best bedd & bedstedle standing in the Parlour Chamber', together with a chest and a cupboard.

One of the overseers was 'my very good freind' John Warden. Ten months later Great Haywards was mortgaged to him for £200. Half of this remained outstanding when he drew up his own will in 1675, and he decreed that the house, in which he had been living when it was mortgaged, should be sold to enable Hardham's executors to redeem the mortgage. The manor he left to his son John, and on his death in 1730 it passed to his son Francis and then to the Sergison family.

Another of Thomas Jenner's cronies remains to be noticed. He is George Alfraye, who was already in his mid thirties when he came to Cuckfield from Hartfield about 1580. In 1593 he was keeping the churchwardens' accounts, and he himself was warden in 1604-5; the parish registers record the burial of a servant of his in 1602. We have a record of his sale in February 1609 of a house, now the Dolphin public house, on the corner of what are called in 1638, Paddock Lane and Mouster Green. At the time it had a barn and garden, and was known as Vynalls, after John Vynal, who had died in 1599. In the centre of the road junction stood the Mouster Oak, and beside it a smith's shop is shown in 1638. When his wife was buried in 1608, Alfraye was described as a 'yeoman & smith'. His successor was Henry Davy, a tailor, who was still there in 1638; clearly he kept up Alfraye's smithy. Davy had lost his wife in August 1610. The following May he married as his second wife Mary King of Butlers Green, the widow of John King, and the couple lived together for 22 years. King is presumably to be identified with the yeoman who in 1576 sold to Thomas Jenner two and a half acres of land on the north of 'the Highway leading from Cuckfield Town to Haywards Heath', with a house that is marked as the manor court house in 1638 and is known today as Steeple Cottage. This appears to date from the fifteenth century.

In 1631 Davy vested the property in his brother Edward in East Grinstead, although he himself continued to live there. But he seems to have passed on by

1654, for the house was then made over to Edward's daughter Sarah and her husband Edward Burtenshaw, a Hurst husbandman.

In 1695 there commenced one of those involved mortgage arrangements that were all too common in the area at that time. With its details we need not concern ourselves, save to note that the house was then occupied by Thomas Divall, and that Richard Hamonds, perhaps a thatcher by trade, had followed him by 1705.

The house was still known as Vinalls in 1809, and the field beside it on the west still bore the name 'Vinals field' in 1843. Its first appearance as an inn seems to be in 1832, when it was known as The Dolphin. The name Sergison Arms appeared by 1845.

We have hinted that the appearance of Muster Green on the manorial map, more clearly marked on the draft Ordnance Survey map of 1794, suggests that it developed over a long period from the passage of traffic, particularly cattle, across the heath; we have noticed that the heath itself seems first to have been named early in the sixteenth century, at about the same time as Sunte and other names in the area. Support for this idea comes from the later spelling 'Moyster', which may well indicate the nature of the ground. It is well known that the state of Wealden roads before they were turnpiked left much to be desired; as late as 1807 it was recognized that Isaacs Lane 'is much out of repair, narrow. and incommodious for travellers'. The agricultural writer William Marshall had commented a little earlier that the Wealden roads 'are the worst in the kingdom': 'formed of pure clay worn into hollows and sloughs' and 'intolerable to a stranger', even in early summer. And all this well after turnpikes had been introduced in the county.

The poor state of Wealden roads was due in part to slackness by local landowners. In May 1614 the occupiers of lands between Bridgers Mill and Polstub were reminded of their responsibilities when they were ordered to clear the ditches along the King's highway, and in 1617 we hear of the misdoings of two men with interests in our neighbourhood: Sir Stephen Boorde, who owned Matthews on the eastern border of the heath, was reported to have caused a public nuisance by dumping logs in Cuckfield town, and George Alfrey (who was admittedly a very old man by that time) was ordered to clear the drain under his tenement. In 1629 we hear of a 'gutter logg' across the road near Scrase Bridge, and of a 'water gullett' emptying into the King's highway towards Balcombe.

The road leading from Upper Ryelands bridge past Borde Hill and Sugworth was also the King's highway, but in the summer of 1649 three Cuckfield men, Abraham Pelland, Alan Gaston and Thomas Burtenshaw, were saddled with the responsibility of repairing it; the first of these had land to the east of the heath, but the others seem not to have had any interest in the area. As the road came to the heath, it passed Bridgers mill over the mill bridge mentioned in 1575. To the east, along the northern perimeter of the heath, lay Millgreen. or Ashurst, Mead, which together with the mill had belonged to Edward Pelland, father and son, between 1588 and 1629 at the least, although the Cuckfield parish registers show that other families were living at the mill shortly after 1600. Towards Scrase Bridge lay (a second) Wigperry Mead and Church Mead.

Because the 1638 map does not distinguish clearly between highways and other roads, it is not possible to decide which path the London road (as it is designated) took in crossing the heath. There was a network of ways across the waste, not all of which are discernible in the present road system. At the eastern end of the present Church Road it joined the road from Lindfield through Scrase Bridge before continuing southwards, probably to follow the path of the later Newchapel–Brighton turnpike, along the road through Wivelsfield that we have noticed in the last chapter, and past Shoulders and Pennies noted in 1638. The first of these perhaps took its name from Roger Sholder of Wivelsfield, who was a juror for Loxfield hundred in 1595; the second survives in Big and Little Pennies in Wivelsfield Road, of which the second (now part of Dinnage's garage) bears a modern sign reading 'Mr. Pennies House 1600'. The name appears in the Wivelsfield parish registers between 1624 and 1647, but the burial of Agnes, wife of Thomas Penny, is entered at Cuckfield and dated 27 February, 1624.

A more interesting road is that running from west to east across the map. We have already noticed that this was known as the road between Cuckfield and Haywards Heath in 1576. In 1638 the King's highway turns to the south east at Isaacs Lane to skirt the demesne of Great Haywards to the south, and continues eastwards to join the Chailey road at a point east of Triangle Road. The route past Butlers Green, however, seems to have been well established. We have suggested that the extension of the waste through Muster Green may have been brought about by the continual passage of animals and carts, and the map clearly designates a path leading north east from there as leading to Lindfield and London. About 1790 the road appears in a view towards Butlers Green as rutted but fenced on the south; but by that date the road had been turnpiked for almost 20 years, and was probably in a far better condition than it had been a century and a half earlier.

The heath itself, however, seems to have changed not at all within that period: essentially the same picture appears in 1794 as in 1638. The northern edge extended, as we have seen, from Bridgers mill to Scrase Bridge. From there it turned south to follow roughly the path of Oathall and Hazelgrove Roads, skirting what are shown in 1638 as 'tenants lands' to the east, and passing a number of more substantial estates on its way. The first of these belonged in 1638 to Alexander Bridges. He had married at Lindfield in 1633 Mary Payne of Cuckfield, and in 1661 he acted as overseer of the will of Nicholas Hardham the younger, for whom the map was drawn up, together with John Warden. He was therefore a man of some consequence, and evidently on terms of some intimacy with the testator. In 1679 either he or his son possessed Wigperry; this was presumably the meadow nearby that we have noticed, since he was a Lindfield man, and in 1723 another Alexander Bridges was party to a release of Bridgers to Walter Burrell.

In 1636 Bridges was rated at Lindfield for Otehall, and his house may be identified as Middle Farm. Further along the road, near the junction with Oathall Avenue, lay Matthews. In 1607-9 Gerard Gatland lived there; because several men of that name were living at the time, it is difficult to discover more about him, but he may well have had a house and land at Pilstye farm on the River Ouse, near the railway viaduct. By 1629, however, Matthews had become the property of Sir Stephen Boord, one of the greatest landowners in the district. But in 1638 'Mr Boord' is shown in possession; Sir Stephen had died in 1630, and had been succeeded by his son George, who had been born in 1607. George survived until 1680, and bequeathed to his eldest son Stephen lands 'called Lullynges, Graylings and Matthews, occupied respectively by John Newneham, Thomas Breete and Thomas Gibsonne' together with other property. It is tempting to think that the holding derived its name from the Richard Mathewe who had hauled another Stephen Borde and others before the Star Chamber for attacking his wife in 1537, but there seems no evidence for this.

Further south again there was Petlands, which gave its name to the later Petlands Wood which in 1794 covered an extensive area between the edge of the parish of Lindfield and the heath. In 1629 there is no sign of extensive woodland. Petlands is said to border on Rowland, and close at hand are 'Newman's land called Veralls and the Gubrides', in an area where woodland might be expected.

We first hear of Petlands in a deed concerning various properties of the Michelborne family in 1568. Thomas Michelborne, of Grays Inn, a son of John, late of Westmeston, is described as owning 'one messuage and certeyn lands, Meadowe lands and Pasture' extending to about 110 acres, of which part was Petlands, which his father had bought from a man in Wivelsfield. The land was described as 'being in Cookfeild adjoyning to Heywards Heath', and as being in the occupation of John Affeld and John Bassett. The first name appears in the Cuckfield return for the 1524 subsidy with a low assessment, one of a number with the same surname; the second was probably a much younger man: the burial of 'ould Joan Bassat wife of John bassat' is noted at Cuckfield in 1606. Later it came into the possession of Nicholas Hardham the younger, who made it over to Abraham Pelland in 1634; in his turn he made it over to John Warden in 1661 after moving to Portslade. Pelland was another man prominent in Cuckfield: he was responsible for the churchwardens' accounts in 1639-40, and seems to have acted as overseer of the will of the first John Warden's widow in 1653, together with Alexander Bridges.

Perhaps the most interesting deed of all relating to the property, however, is dated 1683. It concerns the division of the estate of Isaac Allen of Lindfield amongst his heirs. Petlands was one of the holdings involved. It extended to about 100 acres, and had formerly been occupied by John Walter, who is perhaps the same as the John Walter who married at Cuckfield in 1645 and was buried there in 1679. More recently the land had been occupied by Thomas Davie. Now it was to become the property of James and Mary Fletcher, a London couple, together with 'comon of pasture For all manner of Cattle in or upon the Wast ground or Comon comonly Called Haywards Heath'.

The adjacent land called Rowlands went to another heir, Elizabeth Allen, a spinster also living in London, as part of a holding of 76 acres that included 'Graveleigh, . . . Wards Land, Hurst Meade, parcell of Fowles'. 'Graveley, Lyndefeld' is described as 'lands of Richard Scriven' in the will of Robert Stanford in 1582. Scriven died in 1633/4, evidently a prominent inhabitant of Lindfield; it is interesting to see that John Scriven of Lindfield married an Amy Scrace at Cuckfield in 1625. Rowlands and Wards Land are mentioned in 1592 and 1605 as held of the manor of Franklyns from Ralph Pope, who had a considerable holding in Wivelsfield that included Clevewater. Hurst Mead is perhaps the same as the 26 acres known as Hurstwood linked with 95 acres north of the Chailey road in the possession of Ralph Pope's son Sackville in the following 20 years.

The story of Petlands illustrates the grouping and re-grouping of land holdings that we encounter on the other side of the heath. We should note that in 1794 Gravelye is shown to be well clear of the belt of woodland called Petlands Wood, and it would seem that the land was cultivated less extensively than formerly. But woodland has always been a feature of the Wealden landscape, and the need to conserve it seems to have been widely accepted, perhaps as an aid to the animal husbandry practised in the area.

Another aspect is shown by Peter's Cottage at the end of New England Road. The house was built originally perhaps about the end of the sixteenth century, but was considerably extended about a century later, probably as a result of the occupant's increasing prosperity. It was sold in 1595 by a

Cuckfield yeoman named Thomas Joyner to John Martin, a weaver, together with a shop, barn, hempyard and two crofts, for £60; the holding extended to 4 acres, and was described as part of Gubride bounded on the west by Haywards Heath. Martin was already living there.

Of Joyner we know nothing. Although he retained lands in the vicinity after the sale, he seems to have disappeared from Cuckfield by 1619, since his name does not appear in the subsidy return. Of Martin, however, we have a fair amount of information. The baptisms of two of his children in 1600 and 1604 were recorded at Cuckfield; he was assessed at the modal figure of £20 2s 8d for the 1619 subsidy, the same as the occupant of Boltro Farm on the other side of the heath; and he was buried at Cuckfield two years later. Nevertheless, his interests extended beyond the parish: his heirs were held liable to contribute to churchyard maintenance at Lindfield in 1636, and he held two parcels of land in Chailey, besides a croft of 4 acres near Pilstye Bridge.

Evidently he was also the tenant of land on the heath itself which lay in the manor of Keymer, and which therefore does not appear on the 1638 map. It appears that the enclosure dated from 1562, 80 years earlier than any enclosure recorded on the Hayworth portion. We are told nothing about it save that once it was called Illmans, but probably it was one of the plots shown on the 1794 map lying on either side of the Ditchling road. This suggests that the Keymer portion was less intensively used for the common pasturing of beasts; we must remember that Haywards Heath contributed less than 4 per cent of the total area of waste and common land to the manor. It is possible, however, that Illmans provided some sort of trading outlet for wayfarers; we know that there was a fair on the heath in 1788.

After Martin's death we hear nothing of the Gubride holding until 1630. Then it was sold by his heirs to John Wright, a Lindfield butterman (a dealer in butter); he presumably was a sitting tenant, for he paid only £43, and six months later John Wright junior, probably his son, disposed of the property to Thomas Comber, a Lindfield shoemaker, for £75. This represents an increase in money terms of 25 per cent over 35 years, compared with a general increase in prices of 15.5 per cent over the same period. Since the land changed hands so quickly on the last occasion, we may assume that there was no difficulty over that price. Comber was still there in 1638, although he had been rated in 1636 in respect of other land in Lindfield.

The deeds describing the land tell us that it abutted onto land they call Potlands belonging to John Warden. The 1638 map shows 'Wardens Barne' and 'Wardens house & Lande' towards the end of Franklynn Road, and suggests that he already owned part of the land called Petlands before his son acquired Pelland's holding. Other adjacent land had belonged to Thomas Newnham, who when he died in April 1638 also owned Wickham, shown on the map as outside the Hardham manor, together with property in Wivelsfield, Plumpton and elsewhere; his will shows that he was related to both the Pelland and the Jenner families. He was evidently a considerable local landowner: when Sir Charles Howard had it, probably before 1618; Wickham alone was reckoned to cover 120 acres.

These properties, however, did not account for everyone living on these lands; the Cuckfield parish registers have entries between 1607 and 1612 relating to the family of William Burlie 'of Gubride'. There are entries showing that others were living on, or perhaps beside, the heath: John Whittepayne, 'an ould man', was buried in 1603, for example. The next year was recorded the burial of 'the wyfe of Thomas Hassellgrove the collyere of haywords': the entries for the baptisms of two children in 1608 and 1611 describe him more specifically as 'of Haywards Heath'. Since one of these took place at Wivelsfield, it seems reasonable to suppose that the family lived on the Keymer section or near it, perhaps on the enclosure we have noticed opposite Illmans.

It is always risky to assume identity only because people have the same name, but there are a few interesting hints. The collier on the heath may have been the son of a tailor in Ditchling who was aged 60 in 1597. In 1614 a Thomas Haselgrove was a tenant of the manor of Ditchling of five acres in the parish near a bridge, and in the following year he (or another with the same name) was ordered to repair a bridge in Bolney because he had lands there. The name also occurs as that of a witness to a deed of 1610 relating to lands in Streat. It seems as though Thomas Haselgrove may have been as prosperous as John Martin; unlike Martin, his name is remembered in a street name today.

There are other signs of activity on the Keymer section of the heath; this extended to Colwell Road on the south-east from the Cuckfield boundary aligned roughly with Triangle Road. For evidence of this we turn to a pair of deeds relating to land mentioned at the end of the last chapter, lying beyond Colwell Road. In 1675 Thomas Hurst, who occupied Hurstlands and Brucksparrs, granted the land to a Sevenoaks widow named Margaret Boswell, together with rights of pasture on Haywards Heath. Her conveyance, six years later, of some land in Wivelsfield, included her interest in the lime kiln on the Heath. We come across the kiln in 1809 and 1816. In 1861 it is shown on the site of the present car park south of Church Road.

We have already seen that enclosures on the Hayworth part of the heath dated from the seventeenth century. Ten are recorded between 1642 and 1730; of these two occurred within a year early in the Civil War and three more before the turn of the century and after Hardham's death. We have no means of identifying most of these. One made in 1682 involved a lease for 500 years of the highest point on the heath, on Church Road opposite the site of St Wilfrid's church; a windmill was built by Thomas Comber, a Lindfield miller, and it was still there in 1794.

The timing of the two earliest enclosures is interesting in that between them occurred the only event that gives the heath any military significance. The first major confrontation in Sussex took place about the beginning of December 1642, when Sir Edward Ford, the unscrupulous Sheriff of Sussex, flushed with his own success at Chichester, confronted a smaller Parliamentary force at Haywards Heath. Unfortunately for him, he had been misguided enough to recruit his soldiers by means of threats against their property if they refused to join him. Naturally enough, morale was not what it should have been. His force was routed by the Parliamentarians, and his men fled in the direction of Hurstpierpoint and Ditchling. It seems curious that, in spite of this event, the last enclosure for twenty years should occur within six months while war was still in progress.

Towards the end of the century we hear of the family of another weaver, Richard Burt, who were living on the heath; and there was a yeoman's wife or widow also. In 1717 it was noted that a Presbyterian minister named Thomas Frost was to be found 'at Heward's Heath in ye Parish of Cookfield'.

We know little about these enclosures, but it is clear that they were made in different parts of the heath. We are probably safe in assuming that Mr Frost's house was close to the road at Scrase Bridge, as he served congregations in both Lindfield and New Shoreham; and other land was leased near the Priory estate at Sussex Square (1714) and in the Sydney Road area (1730). Unlike the Keymer enclosures there is no trace of them in 1794 or on the enclosure map of 1861. Some at least were small plots between the Lindfield–Ditchling road and the holding on the eastern side.

On the west the heath was bounded by two farms separated by Muster Green. Of these Great Haywards was the more prominent. We have suggested that this was the original Hayworth that gave its name to the heath; by 1638, however, what had been the manorial demesne had been eroded. The farm was owned by members of the Hardham family as early as 1593, when it was made over to Thomas Jenner and James Hardham, and Nicholas secured the corn tithes in 1599. We have already noticed the financial embarrassment of the younger Nicholas; in 1638 he is shown in possession of both Great and Little Haywards, but in 1651 he made over the farm to Abraham Pelland as security for a mortgage. Over the following 10 years there was accumulated an increasing mortgage debt to Samuel Blunt, a Lindfield mercer. He relinquished his interest in 1662, but then John Warden, whose father had already acquired that part of the demesne that lay nearest to his house at Butlers Green by 1638, gained an interest in the land, and in 1675 he secured the ownership of it.

There followed another series of mortgage negotiations. As a result, the farm came into the hands of Charles Sergison, who was related to the Warden family by marriage, together with Little Haywards, a field abutting on Isaacs Lane, and its associated lands Pellands, Stocklands and Cooks.

We have already noticed a mention of the house now known as Little Haywards in 1607. This was in connection with the Kitchener family, who seem to have left Cuckfield by 1620. In 1591 the house was taken over by Dorothy Garston, the wife of a Cuckfield yeoman, from George Davy, who perhaps had had it for some time previously. Two years later Thomas Jenner gained possession of the house, and in 1605 it was mortgaged to Elizabeth Gorringe of Horsham and her son Henry. It seems probable that these two were the widow and son of William Goring, who died in 1602 possessing extensive property in Mid Sussex and as far west as Petworth and Ferring. It was at this time that Richard and Elinor Kitchener were living in the house as tenants.

The interest of the Gorringes in the house seems to have been short-lived, for in 1612 John Warden acquired it together with its associated lands; they are clearly distinguished by colour on the 1638 map at the eastern boundary of the Hayworth demesne, when it is shown as occupied by Nicholas Hardham. Nevertheless, the whole enclosure remained in the possession of the Warden family until 1712, when it passed to Walter Lucas, a gentleman of Cuckfield, and George Goring of Barcombe. At the end of the century, when Thomas Chatfield was the tenant, there were five fields, amounting to 17 acres of arable and 2 of meadow, with a further 6 acres of woodland and 2 of pasture.

Another encroachment on the Hayworth demesne can be seen on the 1638 map along its northern boundary on the site of the present Victoria Park. This was known as Stanfords when we first hear of it in 1606, and extended to 8 acres. At that time it was occupied by John Gatland, but it was owned by a Cuckfield yeoman named Gerard Bridger, who sold it to a Keymer yeoman named Edward Davyes or Davye, who had another croft of 5 acres in Cuckfield. In 1675 it was reckoned as 7 acres when the family of Robert Banks, who had died in 1668, came to sell it to Joseph Whiston of Lewes. Unlike the Banks family, Whiston seems not to have lived there, for when it came to be sold in 1691 after his death it was occupied by Edward King. He continued as tenant of the next owner, John Chantler, a Newick yeoman, and was still there in 1717, when the 'messuage or tenement, barn, common garden and orchard, and all those lands', amounting in all to 7 acres, were sold to Thomas Hall. When Hall came to make his will, he included a house and land called Bankes 'on or near Heward Heath', and in the 1790s we come across references to 'Stamfords otherwise Stanfords and Bankes'. This is a further illustration of the variety of names by which a piece of land might be known.

Another erosion is shown coloured red on the 1638 map. This is a large plot of ground opposite Vinalls and Butlers Green, which was in the possession of John Warden. The coloration seems to indicate that the land was no longer part of the manor, since the same colour was used for Wickham on the northern edge of the map, which was in Lindfield, for Pennies and Shoulders to the south, and for the eastern part of Cuckfield town on the north western corner, and may be taken as further evidence of Hardham's straitened financial condition.

Beyond this land to the west lay two houses that relate to that period. In Chownes Road lies Chownes, now a modern house, which seems to have taken its name from John Chowne; he is noticed in the perambulation of 1629, but does not appear in the subsidy list of 1621, although his children's names appear earlier in the parish registers. The reference in the perambulation to 'John Chownes inheritance', which had been known as Renfields, suggests that he enjoyed the land for only a short time before he died in 1630, a little more than a year after his wife. In 1638 this house belonged to John Lucas; but later it was linked to Wigperry, which lay around the courthouse (Steeple Cottage), and fell into the hands of Timothy Burrell towards the end of the century. By 1768 both tenements had passed to Francis Warden, and in 1809 they appear in the manor court's list of lands owned by the lord of the manor.

The other house was at Tylers Green, at the junction with Chownes Road. It is clear from the map that Tylers is a corruption of Tylehouse, and the 'tiled house' where John Kinge was living when his son John was born in 1607 would have been the house that still faces towards Broad Street. The description of the house suggests that tiling may have been unusual in the locality, perhaps because the quality of the tiles available necessitated frequent repairs. Kinge was the tenant also of some land at Hatchland, which is perhaps to be identified with Hatchgate; it is interesting to see that in 1638 the occupant of the house also possessed Vinalls.

North of Muster Green the heath was flanked by Boultrowe, a farm of some 30 acres, the name of which survives in Boltro Road. At its junction with Muster Green still stands the farmhouse; but although the house contains traces of medieval building the farm itself cannot be traced earlier than 1590. A point of especial interest is that the area of the farm, as given in its deeds, diminished during the seventeenth century from 30 to 24 acres and thereafter remained stable; but the description of its boundaries remained unchanged: Paddock Lane to north and west, and Haywards Heath to south and east. It seems clear enough that that heath was continuing to expand at Muster Green at that period. The farm seems never to have been profitable; was the subject of an involved series of mortgage negotiations during much of its existence. By 1638 the farm had come into the possession of the Vicar of Cuckfield, Thomas Vicars, and it remained in his family until the following century.

We have mentioned Paddock Lane, as it is called on the map, now Paddockhall Road. It seems always to have marked the boundary of a farm, but as a road leading from Muster Green to the heath it does not seem to have served much useful purpose. However, the map shows that by 1638 there was an access road leading from it to Lucas's, then owned by a man merely named as Edwards. This may have been John Edwards, a ward of the King then aged 6fi, who owned Ashurst Mead near the mill as well as some property called Fields. There were a number of holdings with this name in the parish; if Lucas's was one of them, we may hazard an explanation of the manner in which the house came by its later name. For the boy died in 1644, and his estate was inherited by his aunts.

One of these was Frances, wife of Walter Lucas, a member of a Wivelsfield family, who described himself as of Cuckfield in his will; one of their children was baptized in Cuckfield shortly before his own death in 1657. He seems to have been the grandfather of the man who acquired Little Haywards in 1712, and by then the family was well established in the parish. If the family acquired the house, it is quite natural that it should have come to bear the family name, as occurred so frequently in the area. It seems reasonable that the inheritance of the house was the occasion of the family's move to Cuckfield, although the elder Walter retained an active association with Wivelsfield as late as 1648. The existing house appears to have been built in the seventeenth century.

There were other well established houses in the vicinity of the heath by this period. Occupation at Sunte, for example, can be traced as far as 1522, to a period when many place names first appear: the will of Richard Mascall alias Michelborne refers to 'Sonnte land in . . . Lyndefelde'. The house was in the possession of the Ferralls from 1581 at the latest; when Richard died there, he was followed by his son, John.

The picture that has emerged from this discussion is that of a number of scattered farms and other holdings around the heath and on the borders of Lindfield, Cuckfield and other parishes. There was no nucleated community, and the villages were some distance away. But we sense a communal feeling reflected in the kinship that existed among the landowners and tenants.

Boltro Farmhouse (now The Old House), Muster Green.
Photographed *c*1910.

The Sergison Arms (also known as The Dolphin).
Photograph dated 1906.

26

Muster Green as it is today.

Little Pennies, Wivelsfield Road, now the offices of Dinnage's Garage.

THE RAILWAY COMES

STOCK-jobbers were commuting by coach from Brighton as early as the 1820s, and in 1823 the possibility of constructing a horse-drawn railway between London and Brighton was debated. Shortly afterwards a route for a steam railway through Shoreham was surveyed, with a view to extending the service to Paris; but that project also came to nothing. Thereafter matters rested until the 1830s, when the matter was re-examined with renewed vigour by a number of engineers.

Many routes were proposed. One prepared in 1833 passed through Beeding, West Grinstead and Steyning on its way to Shoreham; another of 1835 passed Pilstye, Whitemans Green and Cuckfield church in getting to Keymer; two others were planned through Henfield and Edburton; another avoided tunnels by passing through Horsham, Nuthurst and Steyning.

The plan that eventually succeeded was prepared by J U Rastrick and the necessary private Act was passed by Parliament on 15 July 1837. It was not the first scheme to pass through Haywards Heath; a year earlier a plan prepared by Sir John Rennie, the builder of London Bridge, followed a similar path. but it failed to get Parliamentary approval after an exhaustive examination by a select committee. Political pressures influenced the course of events in Brighton, even to the choice of site for the terminus between Brunswick Square and the site of the existing station.

Despite its threat to those who profited from the traffic passing along the high road through Cuckfield, evidence presented in 1836 to the select committee of the House of Lords examining a scheme for a London to Brighton railway to pass through Shoreham indicated that a considerable body of opinion in Cuckfield was in favour of the railway. The benefits of railway carriage for goods were realized, and it was felt that the route proposed by Stephenson through Shoreham would seriously threaten the Cuckfield area by depriving it of London-bound goods traffic. The route traced through Balcombe and Haywards Heath was to be preferred from an engineer's viewpoint if a station was to serve the area.

Nevertheless it seems that not all landowners affected by the successful scheme of Rastrick the following year readily made their land available to the contractors. As late as the summer of 1839 it was remarked that each of the contractors at work to the south of the Ouse viaduct 'has not long had possession of the whole of the land', and that progress had suffered thereby. By then agreements had been made for the acquisition of the necessary land, but it had not been plain sailing. 'In some cases the Directors have been compelled to resort to Juries, in consequence of the extravagant demands . . . of the Landowners.'

The coming of the railway disturbed the land of various owners. The Sergison trustees were naturally affected as lords of Hayworthe and Trubwicke, and others were the Earl of Chichester, who had extensive interests in Lindfield, and John Peter Cherry. who lived at Pilstye. One farm touched by the line was Wickham, to the north of the heath. Another more seriously affected was Boltro, which had been farmed since 1803 by Samuel Molineux, described also as a malster, who was a tenant of the Sergison trustees and a man active in parish affairs. Here the line split the farm from north to south, sweeping away two cottages inhabited by Thomas Willett and Henry Carter, two farm workers; the homes of another couple of workers, John Willett and John Streeter, remained undisturbed on the eastern side of the farm by Perrymount Road, and a fifth man, also probably working on the farm, named John Godsmark, continued to live in Dick Turpin's Cottage, on the site of the former police station.

It seems that the prospect of the railway killed the farmer. Probably he had not been very active for some years; but he seems to have still been alive in 1837 when the Parliamentary Act for the railway was drafted. He was dead by the time the Census was taken in 1841, and his will was proved in May 1842. He was succeeded by his son, also Samuel; but very soon he also was dead, for Robert Harmes was at the farm by 1843. He also was active in local affairs, and by 1847 he had moved to another farm on the Sergison estate at Butlers Green. In 1851 a man already in his mid fifties, David Davey, was there; he was to remain for thirty years. But by then the fortunes of the farm were waning, since it seems there was only one labourer. Perhaps Harmes had seen the writing on the wall.

Another farm about five times the size of Boltro to be affected by the railway was Great Haywards. At the time Thomas Broomfield, a 'tenant of the manor', was there, and in 1843 the farm was computed at 154 acres; in 1851 the tenant was Henry Upton, a 48-year-old Cuckfield man, who had three labourers working for him living in the old farmhouse with him and his family, and whose work was shared by two of the daughters of the house. Through the middle of this farm the line ran also.

Haywards Heath station was placed at the southern end of a contracted section of line. It was described as 'the station for the Towns of Cuckfield and Lindfield' in 1840, but it soon became clear that it was to have more than parochial importance. Just before the line was opened early in July 1841, the *Sussex Weekly Advertiser* carried an advertisement informing 'the Nobility, Gentry, and the Public generally' that a stage coach would ply daily between Uckfield and the station 'on the Commencement of the Line being opened by the Brighton Railway Company'. Of the three 'proprietors' who issued this announcement, one was Edward Drawbridge. His name was to become prominent in the later affairs of the town.

The Census taken in the summer of 1841 shows that the railway labourers, or 'navvies', constituted the largest single element in the population at that time. They numbered more than a hundred; but few seem to have been Sussex men, and there were quite a few Irishmen. Others also were involved with the railway: there were an inspector and an engineer, neither Sussex born, a handful of brickmakers and bricklayers, and six 'grocers', who perhaps were running truck shops for the working men.

The presence of two 'police constables' suggests the unsettled state of the community at that time, although they do not seem to have been members of the official county force; this was represented by a constable in Cuckfield. The pair were aged only 20, and perhaps were railway police.

These were in addition to the more settled elements in the community. The farm labourers seem frequently to have been living in accommodation as primitive as that of the navvies. One family was living 'on land' near Gravelye farm, and others are shown as living in open fields. It was quite common also for families in more permanent dwellings to take in lodgers. Henry Penfold presided at the Sergison Arms, and Richard Kennard ran a beer shop for less prosperous members of the community. Kennard was a man of many parts. Four years later he appears as a coal merchant and fly proprietor at the station, with no mention of his former trade. But by 1851 he had become landlord of the Liverpool Arms, which evidently came into being after 1846, and he was still there in 1857, although it seems that he was replaced for a time in the mid fifties.

One man who benefited from the railway was John Bennett. In 1841 he was a 'groser', but by 1843 he had become landlord of the Station Inn. He remained there for at least another 20 years, by which time he also was dealing in coal. By 1855 the family's business interests seem to have reached their greatest extent. His wife Mary Ann was running the station shop, and there were two firms which seem to have had a connection with him: Bennett and Lee, coal merchants, and Bennett and Newnham, timber merchants. There was a timber merchant near the Market Place as early as 1841 named Joseph Jeffery. He is not to be confused with the grocer who was on the heath at the same time; presumably it was he who is shown occupying land to the north of

Little London in Cuckfield by 1843, for although he appears as late as 1857 he is never associated with Haywards Heath in the directories.

Even more noteworthy is Jacob Caffyn, who was at Lucas's in 1841, when his age was given as 64. He seems first to have become prominent locally around 1828, when he appeared at the manorial court as a member of the homage, or jury. In 1843 he is shown not only in possession of Lucas's, which consisted only of a group of buildings with a small plot of land, but also owning the Market Place (including the site of the Station Inn) and the land behind it. He had obtained Lucas's in 1822, and the grant was confirmed in 1851. After his death on 30 March 1854 the farm passed to James Caffyn, a Robertsbridge draper.

Stephen Wood lived at Hanlye, in which Sir Charles Burrell also had an interest; but he also owned the adjacent Gravelye farm and Sugworth, beside the railway, as well as Harlands to the south east, and by 1843 he also was occupying much of Penlands farm, which lay between them.

At Harlands farm Charles Falkner was in charge both in 1841 and in 1851. On each occasion his designation is that of a farm labourer, although in 1843 his name appears with those of Stephen Wood and James Chatfield; Chatfield was a neighbour of Falkner in 1841, but by 1851 he had disappeared. In those ten years William Falkner, probably Charles's eldest son, had married, and had taken over for his family the part of the farmhouse where in 1841 he had been living with three other young men born outside the county, probably also farm labourers. The second son, Charles, also had married, but was still living with his parents as a 'farm labourer' (more likely with the status of farm servant), together with his wife and infant son, and his younger brother Richard. By the time of the 1861 Census, however, the whole family had moved on, and the house was occupied by Richard Packham, described as a 'farmer'. Gravelye also was in the charge of a farm labourer, although the family had changed by 1851, and a similar situation existed at Penlands and at Sugworth, where also there were two separate families in the farmhouse.

There also were lesser men like Richard Berry. His farm of 20 acres was not worth as much as £10 a year, the minimum value entitled to the franchise under the 1832 Reform Act, and his name does not figure in the list of electors; yet his story illustrates the development of the area.

Petland farm lay between Petland Wood and Franklynn Road, just to the west of Colwell Road. Berry, then aged 40, was there in 1841, and is shown in 1843 to have been occupying both the farm and a large detached field extending back from the Priory frontage on Franklynn Road. His family included five daughters and two sons in 1841. By 1851 there were further additions to the household: a boy and a girl, together with a farm servant and an 80-year-old widower described as a 'pauper'. But two of the older girls are not entered, and the children are equally divided: two girls are 'employed at home' and 12-year-old Richard is 'employed on farm', with James and Harriet at school and William under school age. Ten years later only the three youngest children remain; but now there are three lodgers: a carpenter's labourer, a woodcutter, and a 20-year-old bricklayer's labourer named Thomas White, who hailed from Lindfield. By 1871 he was established nearby in Petland Cottages, and his household included two of his labourers as lodgers; he also was employing another man and two boys living elsewhere. Then he was described as a 'carpenter and brickmaker'; eight years later he is a 'builder and contractor'. He was a director of the Haywards Heath Building Society until 1933.

The little farm on which he was lodging in 1861, however, did not prosper. Ten years later there were three houses on the land. Two were occupied by a stoker at the asylum and a laundress. In the third lived James Berry, whose farm had diminished to 10 acres, with his wife, infant daughter, an 18-year-old 'general domestic servant', and his father Richard, whose role was reversed in that he was now working for his son. In 1879 James was described as a 'carman and coal merchant', and Richard is described as a farmer. This must mean that the younger Richard had returned home, for his name continued for some years. By the end of the century James had returned to farming.

There were, of course, others here when the railway came who were not directly involved in agriculture or in local trade. The Turner family was at Bridgers mill, and its members included young Ellis. In 1851 he was living with his young family and a servant in one of the cottages which had appeared between the mill and the railway, leaving the head of the family, John, described as a farmer of 175 acres, in residence at the mill house together with a couple of unmarried daughters and two each of domestic servants and farm labourers. Ten years later the two sisters were still at the house, but Ellis seems to have left and had become a 'cowkeeper'. He survived until 1884, but had left the area earlier.

Finally there were those who had private means, although it is by no means clear that all those described as 'independent' by the Census enumerator in 1841 fell into this category; many were elderly annuitants or even paupers. One man in his eighties who clearly possessed considerable property was Thomas Kennard, who lived at Muster House with his two spinster daughters Elizabeth and Ann. He had had Stanfords as early as 1809, when he appeared at the manorial court as a member of the homage. He had died by 1843, leaving the two sisters well provided for. In addition to Stanfords and Muster House, they had an interest in Penlands farm, and owned further land elsewhere in the parish. Both survived to see the town come into being, to the end living to the south of Muster Green.

There was also a sprinkling of younger people in the leisured class, such as Gibbs Francis Bent, who was at Petland House, a mansion at the corner of New England Road. A little later he moved up the road to Oat Hall (which now houses Barclays Bank Staff Association). By 1843 another member of the family, John, had land in the New England Road area, and in 1857 most of the land to the east of Hazelgrove and Oathall Roads belonged to the family. The name now survives in Bentswood and the Bent Arms hotel in Lindfield.

Before the railway opened in 1841, hopes that the line would be opened in June were frustrated by difficulties experienced in tunnelling. In the event it was opened on 12 July, but only as far as Haywards Heath, 'for the conveyance of passengers, parcels, horses, and carriages', to quote the press announcement, although 'the conveyance of heavy goods and Merchandise' was not to be undertaken before the entire line was opened on 21 September. In the meantime a coach service was provided between Haywards Heath and Brighton for rail passengers, and a weekday service of four trains in each direction was advertised.

We have virtually no information about the station before it was rebuilt about 1880. Comparison of the 1874 and 1896 Ordnance Survey maps suggests that the two layouts were very similar, though it seems that at the rebuilding the platforms were extended northwards; the stations stood slightly to the south of the present site. However, one difference suggests itself from the positions of the Station Inn and the Liverpool Arms. If the former catered for the upper social classes, it is natural to suppose that it stood near the entrance used by the majority of the railway's customers, since in the early days little, if any, provision was made for travellers among the lower classes for whom the Liverpool Arms catered.

We may be confident, then, that originally the station entrance was in the Market Place, and the Census returns tend to confirm this. After 1880, however, the station's entrance for carriages and goods was at the bottom of what is now Clair Road, near the Liverpool Arms. Now the two rows of cottages for railway workers have disappeared to make room for a car park. In the latter half of the century the area was well populated and had a live community, and in 1887 an advertisement in *Kelly's Directory* was proclaiming the existence of a weekly livestock sale ' every Tuesday at 11 a.m.' by a firm of auctioneers 'in their Yard adjoining the Station and Liverpool Hotel'. The Market Place was served by a smaller entrance connected by a subway to the main entrance at the bottom of Station Road, as it then was.

From the outset the railway was well patronized. In a little more than a year after it opened, the *Illustrated London News* for 29 October 1842 noticed a proposed royal visit to Brighton, and commented 'The Court will doubtless travel by the railroad'. All the more disconcerting, therefore, must have been the accident that occurred little more than a week after the entire line opened. On 4 October *The Times* carried a lengthy account of 'a fatal accident which has occurred on the line near Hayward's-heath'. A locomotive attached to the front of a Brighton-bound train at Balcombe was derailed as the train passed through the cutting at Copyhold Hill, causing a sensational accident by the standards of the time. The account is interesting because of the detail it contains concerning the environs of Haywards Heath station. 'The bodies of the dead', we are told, 'were removed to an adjacent public-house.' This may have been the Sergison Arms or the Station Inn, although neither could properly have been described as 'adjacent'. This identification is rendered even less likely by the precision of the next note: 'Kinchin, the guard of the train, now lies in a beer-shop, near the Hayward's-Heath station.' This was in all probability Richard Kennard's shop, later to become the Liverpool Arms. Kennard is described as a 'beerhouse keeper' in 1843, and we have seen that he had been enumerated earlier as such in the Census. But it may be that his was a small shop, for we are told that 'Goldsmith, driver of the auxiliary engine, . . . was removed to some carpenter's sheds in the vicinity', perhaps on the site of the present telephone exchange at the corner of Milton Road.

It did not take local businessmen long to make capital out of the appeal of the railway to the upper classes. Even before the line was opened, the *Brighton Gazette* was carrying on 8 July an advertisement by William Durrant, a Lindfield draper and general dealer, offering 'at a moderate rent' a modern house in Lindfield which he is careful to point out is 'within ten minutes' walk of Hayward's Heath Station House, on the London and Brighton Railway, which will be opened immediately'. The house was a substantial residence that included '. . . four lofty and airy bed rooms, a store closet, two parlours, a large drawing room, kitchen, pantry, wine, beer, and coat cellars . . . a two-stall stable; coach house, with bed rooms over for male servants; poultry yard; piggery; and a large garden.'

Even this impressive list of offices seems incomplete, for one would expect to find a dressing room also in a house of this quality. A glance at the tithe map suggests that the house was in the Scrase Bridge area, since this was the nearest point in the parish with direct access to the station.

It is difficult to say what the effects were of these developments on the area at large. The prospects of regular employment were too uncertain for a man lightly to seek work on the railway, thereby severing his links with the land: and the example of Croydon suggests that the upper classes were inclined to maintain their enthusiasm over the railways at a discreet distance, an impression confirmed by developments at Brighton and elsewhere. It was not long before the railway started to cater also for the lower classes; on 17 August 1843 the *Brighton Gazette* noted a reduction of fares on mixed trains, although the third-class rate quoted would have prevented the labouring classes from availing themselves of rail travel more than very occasionally. A further reduction was made by 1847, however. and season tickets were introduced. Later a fourth, or Parliamentary, class was occasionally introduced, with a fare that still precluded more than occasional use by the least affluent, at a rate of a penny a mile.

By this time the London and Brighton Railway had changed its name. On 27 July, 1846 the company amalgamated with the London and Croydon railway to become the London, Brighton and South Coast Railway Company. This gives us the earliest date by which the Liverpool Arms could have reached its final size, since the building's Clair Road elevation contained a brick bearing the letters LBSC at its eastern end. That the premises were extended considerably was clear enough. The legends 'Wines & Spirits' and 'Ales & Stout' over the doorways at either end suggested a measure of social discrimination among clients, and that at one time trade was in drink for consumption off the premises.

Besides passengers and their effects (which included horses and carriages), the station at Haywards Heath had to cope with a wide range of goods traffic carried by the company, including livestock. But the greatest volume of traffic was in commodities such as bricks, dung, lime, salt, coal and fuller's earth, which together amounted to twice the volume of agricultural produce carried in 1845. These items were probably carried over relatively small distances, often doubtless as part of the trading activities carried on by railway staff on the side. A later example of this is the supplying of flints to the Sussex County lunatic asylum (lately St Francis Hospital) by the stationmaster George Sowton early in 1860. Such commodities as grain, on the other hand, seem to have travelled between 25 and 30 miles. On 26 June 1846, about the time the corn market was started in an extension of the Station Inn, the *Brighton Gazette* reported at length on a discussion in Cuckfield on the corn trade, and on 2 July it reported that a meeting at the Station Inn had agreed that freight charges by the railway were higher than by other forms of transport, and that they inhibited trade. On the market, the paper commented on the following 22 April: '. . . from the commencement this market has never retrograded, and it still holds its priority over any other market in the neighbourhood . . . Within the compass of a few months, it has gained an immense popularity.'

All this activity seems to have had remarkably little immediate effect upon the neighbourhood. In 1848 there is a note of 'the new shop at Haywards Heath in the occupation of Mr Fox', but he seems to have disappeared by the time of the Census in 1851, and there is no other trace of him. A year earlier, in 1847, Francis William Holloway set up as a builder; but he does not seem to have been in the area at the time of the Census in 1851, although he is shown to have been in Cuckfield by *Kelly's Directory*. He seems to have moved into his permanent house in Milton Road by 1853, for in that year we find a rating assessment for 'Mr. Holloway's new buildings at Haywards Heath', and he was possibly in that vicinity in 1861 (it is impossible to be more precise), when his age is given as 35, and he is described as a master builder and agent and a building surveyor, ready for the growth that was shortly to take place.

In 1843, however, the railway company owned little land beyond the site of the permanent way, and even in 1851 there seem to have been fresh opportunities for employment. We have noticed, however, that the railway was considered a selling point in favour of residential development, and its potential must have been explored by such local tradespeople as Thomas Durrant, the Lindfield organ builder whose business had expanded by 1879 to become Durrant's Pianoforte Manufactory, with 'Town Branches at London & Birmingham'.

The expansion of passenger traffic is shown in the following table covering the whole system, and the receipts from goods traffic more than doubled in the same period, although the mail traffic remained virtually the same. The figures are taken in the main from summaries of the railway company's reports as given in *The Times*. These summaries reveal also that the contribution of season and annual ticket receipts to total passenger revenue rose from 3 per cent in 1848 to 6.5 per cent in 1857,

Year	Passengers carried	Percentage increase	Season ticket receipts (£)	Percentage increase
1845/6	971,081		4,747	
1848	2,485,778	156	10,427	119.6
1854	6,339,533	143	32,664	213.36
1856	6,811,904	7.5	33,155	1.5
1857	7,241,077	5.0	33,476	7.0

By 1851 a community of small trading interests had grown up on either side of the line. This need not surprise us; there was no other focal point in the neighbourhood, and we may suppose that small businesses relying on the rapid communication of the railway would be attracted towards the station area. There were, for example, two timber merchants named Thomas Cook and Henry Leigh at the station on the west of the line. They seem to have been recent arrivals; but Cook at least was living in some style, with a household that boasted a governess and two maids. Both men, however, had disappeared by 1855, and in all probability had been replaced by two enterprises: Bennett and Lee, coal merchants, and Bennett and Newnham, timber merchants. It is quite possible that Leigh is masquerading as 'Lee' at the latter date, and it is more than likely, as we have suggested, that Bennett was closely related to John Bennett, who ran the Station Inn, and whose wife Mary Ann had apparently taken the station shop over from Lucy (probably his mother) since the Census was taken; but there is room for doubt, since it was Lucy's daughter who is named Mary in the Census schedule, and John had a sister named Annie at the inn. The shop later became the County Supply Stores, on the site later occupied by Barclays Bank.

Of the various other humble folk who were living beside the station in 1851 one claims our attention. Walter Henton was a 30-year-old wheelwright living beside the station house. He seems to have been in the area for about five years; seven years later we find that he has succeeded Stephen Penfold at the Sergison Arms. The station house, if the arrangement of the later station is anything to go by, stood near the site of the signal box opposite the Station Inn, and in 1843 a building appears in that position. In 1851 a station clerk named James Brook was living there; the station had not yet risen to a station master.

On the other side of the line the land owned by the railway company was a little more extensive, and deep enough to include the site of the Liverpool Arms. In 1851 there was a group of five families beside the public house. Abraham Beard was living in the yard with his family; he was a 'road carter', conveying goods from the railway to their destinations, and his household included a 20-year-old groom from Billingshurst as a lodger. Even at this early period there was a demand for cheap accommodation that catered for the needs of single men whose work depended on the railway; the fly driver who was living in the station buildings had two lodgers.

There was a row of four cottages, probably backing on to the line. These were occupied by railway staff: a labourer, an engine stoker and two porters. One of these last was Benjamin Godsmark, later to follow Richard Kennard as landlord of the Liverpool Arms. Godsmark was a Cuckfield man who, evidently, had moved around to some extent; not long before he had been in Newmarket, and his wide experience in employment would have fitted him to manage the changing trade of the public house.

By 1851 Kennard was a widower in his mid-sixties; as early as 1832 he had owned a house and land in the area. Now he described himself as a victualler; perhaps the two door signs already noticed dated from this time. His household included two sons whose occupations are not given, and who presumably helped in the running of the establishment, and he also had a housekeeper, a maid and a fly driver working for him. By contrast, ten years later Godsmark was described as an innkeeper. His eldest daughter Mary was a barmaid, and James, the son still at home, was a wheelwright's apprentice, and therefore not closely involved in running the inn. There were three boarders, one a railway porter, besides a single lodger, a house painter from Lindfield.

Clearly this was the inn that was provided by the railway company near the station and run by a lessee, although in 1871 there were no boarders or lodgers; but perhaps the Census that year was taken at a slack time. By that time, however, one of the elder sons, John, was working on the railway as a signalman, and was living with his family and a domestic servant in Liverpool Cottage, which seems to have been part of the same building, constituting the extension we have already noticed. James was living nearby, in the significantly named Liverpool Cottages in Sydney Road. He was then a builder employing two men; about 1880 he succeeded his father at the inn.

We may contrast Godsmark's improved status with that of a neighbour in Station Cottages. James Tidy was a railway labourer who seems to have come from Hurstpierpoint. In 1843 he had been living in a little close owned by the Misses Kennard towards the edge of the heath at Muster Green near the site now occupied by Chelsea House. In 1861 he was still a railway labourer living near the inn. He seems to have left the area by 1871.

The increasing prosperity of the Liverpool Arms probably owed something to the policy of railway companies at 'refreshment stations' in providing facilities on either side of the line, although, as we have suggested, its clientele was markedly different from that of the Station Inn, and the inn seems always to have been a private concern. The Arms at one time catered for engine drivers on the down line, but in 1856 the Inn attracted attention of a different kind, when a handbook for railway travellers noted that 'there is a tolerable inn (Bennett's) close to the Haywards Heath station, where carriages may be hired'. A later writer grudgingly admitted that it might have been 'a good inn, for aught I know, in ordinary times', but grumbled that 'the best rooms were all engaged' by one of 'these visitors from London, with their piles of money and unlimited orders for all the best rooms'.

There were few other signs of business activity. South Road was largely a residential area until late in the last century. The peculiar alignment of the buildings between South Road and Hazelgrove Road is noteworthy; the shop itself is a later addition. In earlier days there was access from the building next to it along South Road to both roads, and it seems safe to identify it with Crossways Villa, which had appeared by 1851, much earlier than most of the other houses in the road.

Nearby a grocer had recently established himself. Edward Kennard first appears with his family in 1851. Then in his mid fifties, he had come from Battle, and had his daughter to assist him and a resident baker. He stayed for at least fifteen years, and in 1870 appears Henry Uridge, again with a daughter as assistant but with no resident baker. He had expanded his business to include furniture dealing and estate agency, and was living in Beatrice House, towards the bottom of Lindfield (Hazelgrove) Road. It seems likely that Uridge took over Kennard's business on his death or retirement, but there may be no way of establishing this.

The present Sussex Hotel in Sussex Square, originally known as 'The Volunteer', first appears in 1861 with John Anscombe as its landlord. He was one of a number who were involved in more than one trade, as he was described as both builder and innkeeper.

The rest of the trade in the neighbourhood at this date was negligible. The landlord of the Fox and Hounds in Fox Hill was described in 1861 as a farmer of 24 acres employing two men, and, as if to underline this, his son was described as a 'farmer's son', although he was a man of 21. Otherwise the housing was taken up with farm workers and their families. One boasted a daughter with the unusual description of 'bootleg maker and glover (leather)', and another had a stepson who was a journeyman wheelwright and carpenter.

There was another development in this part of Wivelsfield, however, that had its effect on the town, as we have already noticed. This was the building of the Sussex lunatic asylum on Hurst House farm. The reasons for selecting the site are clear from the guidance given by the Commissioners in Lunacy on 12 November 1846. '1 The Sites ... should be of a perfectly healthy Character'. The open and elevated nature of the site would be especially attractive. '2 The Asylum should be as Central as possible ... in the County or District it is to serve'.

As early as 1849 it had been recognized that the population of the eastern division of the county was inadequate to support its own asylum, and a joint venture was proposed for the two divisions covering the whole county. Also it 'should be convenient with respect to its easy access by Public Conveyances', and the nearness of the railway would commend the site, in addition to its position in the geographical centre of the county. Further recommendations provided that the site should be away from nuisances 'such as Steam Engines' and not overlooked or disturbed by public roads, and that there should be a good water supply and adequate drainage, 'that the baths, water-closets, and buildings in general, may always be kept perfectly clean and free from bad odours', as another authority explained the next year. Further points may have been rather a counsel of perfection for those times, but they show the drift of opinion. 'Space should be allowed for summer and winter exercise. Warmth must be provided for during winter, light for the winter evenings, coolness and shade in the summer', and so on. The buildings should be 'more resembling a well-built hospital than a place of seclusion'.

As early as 1846 plans were in hand to build an asylum to serve either the eastern division alone or the whole county. But for some reason matters dragged on, and three years later the Home Department pressed the urgency of the matter; '123 Paupers from the County of Sussex are confined' in the Bethnal Green asylum, where cholera had broken out, and the distance of home parishes rendered the return of Sussex inmates difficult in the event of an epidemic. In 1850 surplus facilities at a Kent asylum were offered to Sussex.

Notwithstanding this, the *Sussex Advertiser* was carrying an advertisement for a suitable site as late as 6 June 1854. The stipulation was that the site should be 'within two miles of a railway station on the main line, or else in a central position in regard to the two divisions of the county'; at least one site offered met the second requirement, but it was four and a half miles from the station and was 'surrounded with good roads'.

It was not until May 1859 that the asylum's first medical superintendent, Dr Lockhart Robertson, was appointed, and it was confidently asserted that 'patients will be received at the end of the month'. But there were further delays, apparently due to difficulties over connecting a suitable water supply. On 4 June the *Brighton Herald* was making encouraging noises: 'Two or three weeks hence, according to probabilities, the Sussex County Lunatic Asylum will be open to receive inmates'. Nevertheless, on 14 July, the Commissioners in Lunacy felt compelled to administer some stimulation in the shape of a letter pointing out that there were now nearly 200 inmates from Sussex at Bethnal Green. This had the desired effect and the asylum opened its doors on 25 July.

Once open, the way in which it was run met with approval; the visiting commissioners felt that 'its general condition was satisfactory, and evinced great activity on the part of the Medical Superintendent'. Within a short time Bethnal Green was relieved of some of its Sussex pauper lunatics to fill some of the 425 places available.

Despite the stimulus to local trade the institution offered, and the active part its staff took in local affairs, the birth of the town was not yet. The asylum's letter books show that such local men as Bennett, Berry, Henton and Peirce were being paid in 1859-60, as well as Edward Newnham (as a timber merchant) and Stephen Kent of nearby Pesthouse farm in Lindfield in 1861; and that the asylum was calling at that time upon the services of other tradesmen as far away as Ditchling, Uckfield and even Banstead. We have already noticed that George Sowton, the stationmaster, was being paid for supplying flints at this time. All this suggests that local resources were proving inadequate for the demands of the institution.

Market Place, undated photograph. The Station Hotel is on the left. The cattle market is in the background.

Market Place, north. Undated photograph. The building contained Warnett's stores. The sign of the auctioneer Scott Pitcher was opposite his office next to the bank in Boltro Road; he was active at the turn of the century.

Station Road (now Clair Road), *c*1902. One of the entrances
to the railway station may be seen at the end of the road.

Austens Hotel, the 'commercial and temperance hotel'
run by George William Austen early in the century.

The County Lunatic Asylum (lately St Francis Hospital).
In 1890 it became the asylum for the borough of Brighton.

Telephone Disaster Haywards Heath
January 8th 1908

The Congregational church in Wivelsfield Road,
1961-1915. Photographed in 1908

43

Above, a brick in the wall of the Liverpool Arms, against Clair Road, bearing the letters LBSC (London Brighton and South Coast Railway.

The Liverpool Arms, demolished in 1997. Photographed in 1991

The present United Reformed (formerly Congregational) church in South Road. Built in 1915.

THE TOWN GROWS

T HE town of Haywards Heath did not start to develop until the early 1860s; the building of St Wilfrid's church in 1862-5 provides a convenient starting point for any study of the town as an organism. Thereafter developments were rapid. The population increased dramatically; in 1861 the Sussex antiquary Mark Antony Lower had remarked, 'Haywards Heath . . . has become a centre of civilization and commercial activity', and on 25 April the Cuckfield vestry had ordered the assessment for rating purposes of 'the various new Properties at Haywards Heath'.

The growing importance of residential (and probably commercial) property at this period is demonstrated by the second table in the appendix on page 59; there is no clear indication of the part played by Haywards Heath in this, but we may be confident that it was substantial. The first table gives an indication of social development; an early instance of the attraction of the leisured classes to the district is the seven year lease of Clyde House in St Wilfrid's (Church) Road in February 1862 by a Brighton builder named George Head to a couple of Horsham spinsters, Susanna and Cornelia Neale, sisters of the hymnologist John Mason Neale. At that time there was little sign of development in the road. A year earlier only three families were there. One of them was that of Henry Head, a Horsted Keynes man described as a 'proprietor of houses'. Very likely he was George's father, and thus had a vested interest in the development of the land; for George had already secured the sites of Clifton Terrace and Fairlawn at either end of the road, although the latter was not developed until after the building of the church. He also secured the house that may have been Crossways Villa in 1851.

The situation at the beginning of the decade was one in which potential energy was awaiting the opportunity to be released into urban development. The reason why this had not happened earlier must be traced back to 1806, when Warden Sergison drew up his will. The details of the settlement of the estate were not finally settled until a private Act of Parliament was passed in 1853. Thereafter matters progressed. The enclosure of Haywards Heath was sanctioned under the general enclosure Act of 1858, and the details were settled by an award at the beginning of 1862.

The schedule to the award demonstrates widespread interest. Both local people and more distant men are included. As well as Thomas William Best, a

Cuckfield brewer, James Ellis, a Lindfield innkeeper, Charles Knight, the Cuckfield ironmonger, Daniel Knight, also a Cuckfield tradesman, and the Reverend R E Wyatt, who was to be the first vicar of St Wilfrid's, There were Stephen Peirce, a Cuckfield farmer already living in Church Road, a Brighton timber merchant named George Sawyer, a hatter named William Hart, also of Brighton, and George Head; and there was Thomas Gower, a contractor of Dudley, Staffordshire, who was allotted a plot of land to the north west of Crossways Villa, but whose name survives in Gower Road on the opposite side of South Road, although this was developed much later.

In the earliest stages of the town's growth, two names are especially prominent. The first of these is Richard Pannett, the head of the third family already in Church Road by 1861. By then he was already aged 43, with a prosperous business as a carpenter employing six men and a boy. He had married comparatively recently, for ten years earlier he appears as a farm bailiff living with his cousins, the Kennard sisters.

Ten years later the Census describes him as a builder employing 29 men and three boys, one of whom was his own son Arthur, later to become an architect and surveyor. He had already been described as a builder in 1862, and in 1865 he obtained the freehold of the plot of half an acre 'whereupon formerly a Windmill was erected which has been long since taken down'. to be replaced by his own house. In 1881 the Haywards Heath Horticultural Society met on 'R. Pannett's meadow, South Road'. This was presumably the land that he had bought at the beginning of 1878; it extended to more than 5 acres to the east of the railway and lying north of Great Haywards Wood, on what is now Victoria Park, and the deed includes a restrictive covenant against 'dangerous trade' or nuisance on the land. Exactly ten years later he extended his property to embrace part of the wood to the west of the railway, under similar covenants, but with the interesting addition that there should be no 'Institution for Infectious or contagious diseases' on the land. Clearly the Sergison trustees were apprehensive of the spread of urban development as well as of the old man's interests in building, although the deed describes him as a 'gentleman', with the implication that he had recently retired from the business he had built up in Church Road.

Another man with a much greater stake in the development of the town was Thomas Bannister. The surviving records of his business open in 1866, but it seems that he did not really get started until the following year. By 1871 he had established himself at Limehurst, which lay between Boltro Road and Paddockhall Road, with its access drive almost opposite the junction with Lucastes Avenue; the house was sufficiently important to be mentioned in the description of the enumerator's area, 'Mr Bannister's villa including the servants' dwelling over the stables', although the servants' accommodation at the time was occupied only by a gardener/handyman with his family.

According to the Census return, Bannister was a Cuckfield man aged 29. He seems to have regarded himself primarily as a farmer with 158 acres and employing (as an absentee) five men and two boys. We may make a pretty shrewd guess at the land he farmed. In 1832 the name of John Bannister appears among the Cuckfield electors as the occupier of 179 acres at Sparks, Courtlands and Denmans farms to the north of the village; he was still there in 1841-2, when the occupier of Beech farm, between Whitemans Green and Slough Green, was named Thomas Bannister, the same as a Lindfield farmer who appears briefly in the mid-1850s. John disappears from view in the early 1840s, and it may well be that our Thomas took over the bulk of his land.

Evidently in the early years he regarded his activities as auctioneer and estate agent as of secondary importance; perhaps the shadow of Edward Drawbridge at Scaynes Hill was enough to deter him from relinquishing his farming interests. But from the beginning he attracted established local folk as clients. In 1867, for example, we find Edward Newnham, the builder of Haywards Heath, who may possibly have been involved with the business of Bennett and Newnham 10 years or so earlier; Edward Waugh, the Cuckfield solicitor who was to take a prominent part in local affairs; and Charles Callow, a Cuckfield butcher. In March 1868 we find that he valued the effects of Richard Berry at Petlands farm in anticipation of transfer of the farm to his son, and there were dealings also with Mrs Roberts, the widow of a retired farmer at Holly House nearby, in 1869, and with Mr W Henton, of Haywards Heath and Wickham.

By 1878, however, he was describing himself simply as an auctioneer, for he is described thus in the deed by which he obtained the freehold of a four acre plot of land fronting on to the south side of Triangle Road and to Sussex Road. By 1880 his activities were widespread and his prominence considerable. He started the cattle market in the mid 1860s, and by 1879 he was advertising himself as 'auctioneer, valuer, and estate agent, Haywards Heath'; the business did not move to its final site until 1883, and the pair of cottages already on the site were still clearly identifiable in the firm's premises. By 1887 he had come to own the market; probably he gained control of it at the time of the move to the Market Place premises. But he continued to live at Limehurst, and he extended his land there in 1887 northwards towards the police station. He seems to have lived there throughout the rest of his life.

Despite the success of the business, there are signs that Bannister attempted to diversify his business interests towards the end of his life. In 1899 we find a mention of 'Thomas Bannister, brick maker, Balcombe road', which may relate to a subsidiary activity; in 1907 we find in the same position in the directory entry for Haywards Heath, immediately after the name the firm, comes a clear reference to the old man as a farmer. But this return to his early life was short-lived, for he died in 1912.

Naturally enough, Bannister and Pannett were not the only local tradesmen to shift to the town in its early days. Another who did so was Charles Callow, the Cuckfield butcher we have met already. He was probably a member of the same family as John Thomas, landlord of the Red Lion at Lindfield in the mid 1850s, and John, shown as a veterinary surgeon in 1858 practising in both Cuckfield and Lindfield. Charles had his business 'opposite Station' in 1879; but he was described as a Cuckfield gentleman when he bought property in Station Road during 1883. By the end of the following year, however, he was in St Leonards, once again as a butcher.

Another local man whose interest in the town was even earlier was the first postmaster, Alfred Curtis. As early as 1845 he was in Cuckfield as a grocer and draper and an insurance agent. By the beginning of 1862 he seems to have been established at Muster House, at the corner of Paddockhall Road; but the Census entry for the house in 1861 shows the householder as John Curtis, a retired farmer, as in 1851, with the addition of a grandson and a middle-aged assistant to run the business in Alfred's absence. Indeed. although he may have lived in the house, Alfred's real interests seem to have lain elsewhere; within a short time John, probably his father, seems to have died, and in 1865 the shop and house were leased to Henry James Green, another Cuckfield tradesman, for 14 years.

By 1870, however, the premises had changed hands once again, and the postmaster was John Meux, who seems to have come from Hove, bringing with him his own telegraphist. Meux remained after the expiry of the lease, for he was still there in 1887.

Another local man whose trade was not directly concerned with property development but who moved into the new town was Frederick Whall. He had arrived in Boltro Road by 1878, and had set himself up as a hairdresser and picture frame maker next door to the Pure French Wine Company. His trade coupled with the unusual spelling of his surname leaves little doubt that he was related to, and probably the son of, the Lindfield hairdresser John Whall, who is noted as early as 1845. By 1882 the shop was known as Whall Brothers, but five years later the business had reverted to Frederick alone as a hairdresser. At the end of the century he had establishments in Boltro Road and South Road, but early in the new century he had settled at 16 Boltro Road.

A better example of by-employment is provided by Alfred Willmot, the teacher in charge of St. Wilfrid's school by 1866. The school log-books give no reason to doubt that he was efficient and conscientious; yet he found time to devote to a number of outside activities. He acted as an enumerator for the 1871 Census (it was not unknown for a local schoolmaster to act in this capacity); he says of himself that he was aged 27 and was born in Croydon. He was then living in Stanford Place, with his wife, two infant daughters and a domestic servant, and with his assistant, Emma Leonard, as a lodger. Within 7 years his activities had proliferated. In 1878 he appears as collector for the Urban Sanitary Authority and manager of the gasworks, and by the following year he had moved to St. Hilda's Cottages in South Road, and under the grandiose title 'Alfred Willmot & Son' was advertising himself as 'Coal, Coke, and Wood Merchants'. By 1882 he had left the school.

Others appeared briefly upon the scene, or made little impression. There were Henry Procter, for example, who sold beer at the Queen's Arms in Paddockhall Road during the early 1860s, and Joshua Jones, who ran a similar business at The Star on the Broadway, with a small shop at the Muster Green end, for over 20 years from the mid 1860s. There was George Matthews, who apparently combined the roles of butcher and farmer between 1862 and 1870; and James Ellis, who had a stake in the enclosure of the heath, was at The Triangle in Sussex Road, working as both builder and publican in 1870-1.

Other tradesmen that we have met already in connection with the enclosure award were Charles and Daniel Knight of Cuckfield. Daniel was already in the vicinity of the Market Place when the 1861 Census was taken, but had moved to Sydney Road ten years later, when he was in his mid-sixties. Charles, the ironmonger, moved to South Road about 1870. He is shown as a bachelor in the Census return the following year, where his age appears as 66. But this is probably a mistake, for he was still in South Road in 1887.

Stephen Peirce, the farmer living by the church site in 1861, has a more interesting later history, He was already in his early fifties, but by the following year he had forsaken farming to become a timber and coal merchant, a further indication of the urban trend in the area in the rising demand for domestic heating fuel. By 1871 he had been joined in the business by his son, also Stephen, and the family was living at Oakfield House in Perrymount Road. The elder Stephen, however, seems to have died by 1878: there is no entry for him in the directory that year, and in the following year there is an entry for 'Mrs Pierce' at 6 Oakfield Terrace, probably adjacent to her old home.

This is not the last we hear of the name, however, for in 1882 it reappears as that of a butcher in the Market Place. This must have been the younger man, by then in his early forties, who seems to have become disenchanted with his father's old business. He continued at least until 1907, when the business seems to have prospered sufficiently for him to take his son into partnership.

There is another shopkeeper in the Market Place at that time that deserves to be mentioned. This is Dennis Warnett, who by 1870 had become a grocer at an address given as 2 Market Place. A photograph enables us to identify the site of the shop as the one now occupied by Barclays Bank, with the Station Inn alongside: in all probability this was the station shop formerly run by the Bennett family. In 1871 the shop was next to a butcher's run by a Somerset widow named Jane Stone, and Warnett, then 29, lived there with his wife and an assistant. In 1879 he was advertising himself as the Tea Warehouse and as a family grocer, draper and provision merchant, and assured the public that he supplied 'everything usual in the trade', in the face of fresh competition in Commercial Square from the grocer's and draper's shop set up by Frederick Herbert Beeny on the corner of Sydney Road and Mill Green Road.

Mr Beeny was already proclaiming his establishment to be a 'noted drapery, outfitting & boot warehouse', in which he 'begs to call attention to his large Stock of all kinds of Goods' relating to outfitting, and 'first-class grocery & provisions, ironmongery & earthenware'. This hyperbole appears to have been justified, for the store became known as the 'Sussex emporium', and served the surrounding villages, with trade remaining at a constant level throughout the week. The premises included a post office, and covered an area much larger than any other local shop. Trade prospered until the first World War; but it then suffered a setback from which it never recovered.

Another sign of prosperity at Commercial Square was the appearance around 1871 of the Burrell Arms. Its first landlord seems to have been Ebenezer Hide, a Chiddingly man then in his mid-twenties, described in the Census return as a licensed victualler, who was there alone with his wife. The couple had disappeared by 1878, and Frederick Ferguson, a former railway porter, had taken over. By then trade had expanded; an advertisement of 1879 proclaimed Ferguson to be a wine and spirit merchant (despite the proximity of the Station Inn and the French Wine Company at the top of Boltro Road) as well as a coal and coke merchant, and that there were 'good beds and sitting room'.

Ferguson's involvement in selling coal was in partnership with Benjamin Godsmark, and their yard lay alongside the railway line near the Liverpool Arms. As early as 1852 'the Sawhouse and Timber yard at Haywards Heath station' had been rated, and the yard is shown on the enclosure map to have extended between Station Road and Commercial Square. Later the enterprise became known as Ferguson and Son.

Agriculture, of course, still played a significant part in the life of the town. On 14 February 1883 it was ordained that Haywards Heath should be one of the five towns in Sussex (the others being Brighton, Chichester, Lewes and

Horsham) to submit weekly returns under the Corn Returns Act of 1882. Bridgers mill had been taken over by William Jenner with his son in 1856, and by 1861 they were joined by George W Bailey, who was living in or near the Market Place. The business was primarily flour and grist milling, but it was discovered that steam power was needed to supplement the low pressure of available water to the existing machinery.

Bailey seems to have left the business by 1866, although he continued to live in the town; in 1881 he was living at Grants House in Church Road. William Jenner sold the mill to his nephew Samuel in 1877, who in turn took into partnership a young man named Caleb Higgs, whose father had been a dairy farmer on a large scale in Surrey. In 1880 the partnership quit Bridgers mill for Deans mill. Lindfield. which was leased for 21 years. But the machinery the millers installed was soon outdated; the lease was not renewed, and the partnership restricted its activities to factoring.

In the same year (1880) the partnership rented a timber and slate building that rose to four storeys. It stood beside the railway line below the site at the bottom of Boltro Road later to be occupied by the Capital and Counties Bank (now Lloyds Bank) from 1889; this and the sub-branch of the Brighton Union opened under Edward Waugh in the Station Hotel in 1878 were the first two banks in the town, further indication of the prominence achieved by the station area in the town's commercial development. The Jenner and Higgs building was destroyed by fire in 1915. but a year or two earlier the business had returned to Bridgers mill, and a depot had been opened at Balcombe.

Two further features in the development of the area remain to be noticed. In 1874 a brewery was standing at the bottom of Mill Green Road, at a spot that was later to become the junction with Queens Road. This enterprise belonged to W H Power and Company, who advertised themselves as of Burton-on-Trent, although there was a Willoughby Hamilton Power living in Lewes Road in 1879. The business seems to have closed down in 1882; instead, the Burton brewers Ind Coope had stores advertised as being at the station, supervised by Charles Golding of the Station Hotel.

Further up Mill Green Road, the gas works had stood alongside the railway embankment since 1866. By 1870 there was a resident manager, a Gloucestershire man named George Alexander, who had, as boarders, a middle aged pensioner and his wife.

Brickmaking was another industry in the town. As early as 1849 there is a rating assessment for 'Mr Sergison's new Brickyard at Haywards Heath', and two years later the assessment was increased from £4 to £5, thus suggesting an increasing prosperity for the enterprise. This is probably to be identified with the brickfield that lay back from Sussex Road opposite the junction with

Triangle Road, although in 1874 there was another field opposite Heath Villa (later Chestnuts) in Hazelgrove Road; at one time there was also a smaller yard at Lucas's.

The impression that the Sussex Road site was the principal one is suggested by two entries in the 1851 Census labelled 'Brick Field' apparently relating to that area, although the families enumerated were those of a sawyer and of a journeyman carpenter, and by the appearance in 1861 of a brickyard labourer and a journeyman brickmaker in the Census returns for that area; in 1874 another field, together with a kiln, is shown lying behind the Sussex Road field, in the corner of Ashenground Road and a track that later became Haywards Road. In 1862 the Haywards Heath Brick Works was under the management of William Ashdown; but all trace of it disappears after 1866, and the manager himself seems to have left the town at that time.

The Sussex Road area still had its brickyard workers in 1871. But by then the area showed signs of development; we have already noted the existence of the Congregational church in Wivelsfield Road, and the establishment of the Primitive Methodists just below the Sussex Hotel in 1876 seems to confirm the impression that the lower orders to whom these churches might be expected to appeal were concentrated in that area.

But these churches attracted members from a distance. One was Charles Clarke. the printer in Boltro Road. He was one of the two original officers of the Primitive Methodist chapel, and was generous enough to give five pounds to its funds in November 1876, before the building was opened. He continued his contributions until 1897, although he joined the Congregationalists in February 1882. To both congregations he gave unstinted help; although he remained for only a year in his original Methodist position, he assumed many roles and duties.

He was asked shortly before Christmas 1877 to approach a preacher in Brighton with a request that he should fill the place left by a departed minister, and he became one of four class leaders in the society. In March 1879 he was thanked for his 'persistent effort' to reduce the outstanding debt on the chapel building, and three months later he undertook to oversee 'certain alterations' to the gas fittings in the building. He was a delegate to the District meeting in March 1880; soon afterwards he was almost persuaded to leave the congregation, apparently through dissatisfaction with the financial state of the chapel. His decision to quit the Connexion was finally recorded on 7 June 1881.

His membership of the Congregational society is more fully documented, and evidence of his active participation may be seen on the foundation stone of the present United Reformed church in South Road that he laid on 9 December 1914. We have details of his circle who joined the congregation with him. One was a printer (probably an employee, though this is not stated) named Woodcock, who lived in Franklynn Road. Mrs Woodcock was admitted to membership a month later; since reports on her life and character were offered, she apparently was not already a member of a congregation, and we may guess that she was influenced by Clarke; we notice that the couple were transferred to the Primitive Methodists in Oxford when they left the next year.

From the outset Clarke immersed himself in the church's life. He was clearly already well known to the church elders, for immediately after joining he agreed to visit two members who had been absent for two years. Early in the following January he was nominated as a deacon, and he was one of the two nominated to call on another absentee, a Mr Crichton, the steward at Franklands, who was a member of four years' standing. Later he was to assume control of the church's affairs on the departure of the minister, and chaired meetings in 1884-5. The measure of his authority is further indicated by a note of a meeting of the Sussex Home Missionary Society in 1887: 'The Minutes were not read, as Mr Clarke was unable to attend with them'.

It may be added that he was not the only member of his family to serve the church: his daughter Mary Ann was organist for five years before her marriage at the age of 21 to a Brighton grocer named Ernest Dudeney, and fulsome thanks to her were recorded in the church minute book on 2 October 1889. She was succeeded by her sister Ada.

A later arrival in the new town was George Hilton. His record of service, both to the Primitive Methodist chapel to which he remained faithful until his death in 1938 and to the community, was no less impressive. He was born near Eastbourne, but evidently came to the town from Hastings. He arrived in Haywards Heath in July 1882. with little money but with a bag of tools. For eight months he settled at Crossways (now Sussex Square), and in the following year he invited a lady to join him as his first employee. By 1887 he was settled at Acton House in South Road, described as 'cabinet maker and furniture warehouse'. Business had prospered sufficiently for him to take a displayed advertisement in *Kelly's directory* that year. The following year he moved to premises on the site of the firm's last showrooms on the north side of South Road (which were opened in 1932).

Like Charles Clarke, Hilton gave liberally to church funds. In 1893 he promised £5 to the chapel's jubilee fund, but the usual contribution was £1, and no one else gave more than the minister's £3. He also chaired meetings. and held offices in the chapel, including that of secretary and treasurer for an uncertain period to 1910, and chairman of the trust from 1913. He also was actively involved in leading the services. He succeeded Thomas Lenton, of the asylum, as 'harmoniumist' in June 1886, when he agreed to form a singing class, and there are frequent mentions of him conducting worship at this period. The influential position he eventually achieved is sufficiently indicated by his election in 1914 as secretary and treasurer of the chapel trust as well as organist.

Another tradesman who made his appearance in the area about this time was Cornelius Woolgar, although we cannot discover exactly where he worked. He described himself as a blacksmith or shopkeeper – it is possible that he may have run two separate businesses. By 1887, however, his name is replaced by that of Mrs C Woolgar as a shopkeeper in Wivelsfield Road, and it seems that his widow had taken over. It is possibly she who appears in 1899 as Mrs Charlotte Woolgar, a dressmaker in Gower Road. One can only speculate on what had happened; it is quite possible that the lady was no longer capable of running the shop but still had need of a livelihood. But the matter is complicated by the entry in the Census returns of 1871 of another man of the same name who was a fly driver living in Perrymount Cottages. The name suggests that he was the son of the Wivelsfield Road smith, the more so as he seems to have arrived in the district at about the same time as we first notice the blacksmith, and his wife's name was Charlotte.

Even by 1874 there was no building between the top of Haywards Road (which was then incomplete) and Stanford Place on the south side of South Road and the church school on the north. On the site now occupied by Lloyds Bank stood Canton and Victoria Cottages. On the opposite side, below the site later taken by George Hilton, stood a terrace of four cottages. Lower down there was a second terrace that later became a row of small shops. There was also a pair of shops with living accommodation called Southdown Villas. The ironmonger in one was Charles Knight. whom we have already met, while the other was occupied by a shoemaker named Thomas Ockenden, a Wivelsfield man with a trade much in demand, who seems to have arrived around 1870. By 1874 development had started on the south side of the road with the appearance of Laurel Cottages, a pair of semi-detached houses near Canton and Victoria Cottages, and some buildings had appeared at the crossroads; by the end of the century this side of the road also was lined with buildings; most were small businesses.

In the early 1870s development in the area of Sussex Road was concentrated within the confines of The Triangle, as the stretch of road lying below The Volunteer (or the Sussex Hotel) was known, where the Primitive Methodist chapel was to be built in 1876, although further south the New Inn below the Congregational church, and the Asylum Arms, which probably lay near the junction with Asylum Road (now Colwell Road), both appear as early as 1861; but the latter was only a beer shop, and seems to have disappeared by 1874. The Fox and Hounds also appears as early, but curiously its occupant,

Nathaniel Randall, is described as a farmer of 24 acres employing two men in the Census return, although he appears to have become an innkeeper by the mid 1860s.

An interesting feature of the household at The Volunteer in 1871 is that it included a woman in her mid thirties listed as a servant and described as a dressmaker. The occupation was one that commanded low wages and was regarded by working-class women as an alternative to factory and similar work. The woman was married, and presumably had been brought to the town by her husband; as the house seems to have had no other staff at the time, we may take it that she assisted in the work of running the pub. But that she was described as a dressmaker suggests that this was her principal occupation. A few doors away there was another young woman in the same occupation. Perhaps there was no shortage of work, although many wives in neighbouring households had apparently no gainful employment.

We have already noticed that at that time brickyard workers were still living in the neighbourhood. The Census gives details of them: a brickmaker and a labourer lived next door to each other just below the pub, and a journeyman bricklayer lived down the road with his son, another labourer; and yet another labourer and a bricklayer were in Triangle Road. For the most part the folk living in the Triangle were just working people, but there were exceptions. A draper's assistant, for instance, is found lodging with a bricklayer's labourer; she was not a local girl, and she may well have been working for Henry Uridge at the bottom of Lindfield (now Hazelgrove) Road.

By the site of the later Primitive Methodist chapel stood a baker's shop, where the household included a resident assistant and the widow of a grocer as a lodger. Next down the road came a terrace of six cottages. of which the last was the greengrocer's shop of Samuel Ockenden. probably Thomas's younger brother. A basketmaker lived in the next pair of cottages, next to an elderly couple described by Willmot as 'helpless (old age)', who seem to have been cared for by their daughter-in-law, described as a charwoman although she also had a year-old son to look after.

Beside the Triangle Inn stood three shops. The first belonged to a butcher named John Holman. who had a resident assistant; the second was run by the son of James Ellis, the landlord of the inn. In contrast to Jacob Grist of The Volunteer, he had a large family, five of whom were of school age or younger; the sixth, a girl of 12, had already left school and was working as a barmaid. The third shopkeeper, another baker named James Daws, was still there in 1879; but all the others had moved away, with the exception of Ockenden. His brother was also at his old address.

In Triangle Road there stood Waterloo House, a general stores presided over by Albert Thwaites. a 29 year-old Brighton man whose household rose to two servants: a nurse to care for his infant son, and a domestic servant. The grocer's shop further along the road included a nursemaid, but with more justification, for the husband was an attendant at the asylum, and it was his wife who ran the shop, although she had two small children with her. Neither of these shops was in the same hands in 1879. A young Hampshire butcher named Charles Jeffery, who was living in the road in 1871, had apparently moved to Wivelsfield or Sussex Road by 1879. His neighbour, a Norfolk basketmaker named William Farman, had disappeared by the end of the decade, as had Herbert Smith, the Wiltshire tailor three doors farther on.

There was therefore a definite disinclination to settle in this area, even among the tradesmen, at least in early days. The density of settlement in the Triangle was rivalled only in Station Road, with its housing for railway and ancillary workers. There were large houses in Franklynn Road which would have needed the services of workers from outside, and the asylum clearly had a large number of non-resident staff.

Furthermore, even in 1871 there were two small private schools in that part of the town. Henry Hudson, described as an agricultural commission agent, had half a dozen youngsters in the charge of one schoolmistress, aided by his daughter as a pupil teacher, at Western House; and at Laura Cottage, a little way up Hazelgrove Road, an assistant curate at St Wilfrid's, one James Horam, had a similar establishment, apparently under his own supervision. In this instance, however, the scholars numbered five, ranging in age from 9 to 25, three from overseas. Such an establishment can hardly be reckoned to have been a credit of the community.

Another feature in the town's development should be mentioned. This is the foundation of the Haywards Heath and District Permanent Benefit Building and Investment Society in 1890. It was by no means the first society in Sussex; the Hastings and Thanet had been founded in 1849, the Rye Benefit in 1851, the Horsham Permanent Benefit in 1856, and the Lewes in 1870, for example, even the Mid Sussex had been in existence for ten years.

The first meeting was held at Edward Waugh's office in Boltro Road on 16 July. The record of attendance reads like a roll-call of the most prominent names in the town's early history: E and E J Waugh, T Bannister, F Ferguson, C Golding (the landlord of the Station Inn), T White, C Clarke, F Whall and Holloway are among them. Of these Bannister, Golding, Clarke and White were on the first committee, together with Major Maberly of Cuckfield and others.

E J Waugh became the Society's first solicitor when it was constituted on 21 November 1890, and Charles Mackenzie became its secretary. For reasons that are not clear, Mackenzie was dismissed in September 1895, and after eighteen months Harry Plummer succeeded him after acting as an agent for the Society. He had his office at his own house, Lyntonville in Hazelgrove Road, and served the Society for forty years.

George Hilton's shop at Acton House, South Road, during the 1880s. The figure on the right is probably Mr Hilton.

Appendix

1 Social stratification of Haywards Heath in 1851, 1861 and 1871

The following analysis is of a systematic sample of heads of households returned in the enumerators' books from the Censuses of 1851-71. The return for 1841 does not lend itself to this type of examination, and in any event the structure of the population at that time is distorted by the presence of a considerable number of men connected with the construction of the railway.

	1851	1861	1871
Leisured and property class			
With domestic servants	2	4	16
Without servants (eg retired, widows)	3	10	17
Professional class			
Clergy, doctors and others	-	-	9
Schoolteachers so designated	-	-	7
Businessmen			
(perhaps with interests elsewhere)	-	1	12
Farmers	6	8	13
Communications			
Railways: skilled and white-collar			
workers	11	7	21
labourers	5	1	-
Road transport	7	4	11
Tradesmen			
Innkeepers and victuallers*	3	4	6
Shopkeepers	2	1	24
Others	4	8	22
Lunatic asylum staff	-	3	5
Artisans	20	17	69
Domestic servants**	3	2	15
Labourers	14	16	40
Paupers	2	-	1

* *The distinction seems to indicate the facilities offered by the establishment. Innkeepers offered accommodation; victuallers ran taverns, the Victorian counterpart of the modern restaurant.*
** *Resident domestics of course are excluded.*

2 Rateable values of property in Cuckfield, 1861-75

The following figures, taken from the minutes of the Cuckfield Local Board, suggest the changing values placed on various types of property within the parish of Cuckfield. The amounts have been translated into decimal currency values. It will be noted that the first category was the only type to increase in value; this suggests the increasing average prosperity of the inhabitants. In the ten years 1861-71 the population increased by a quarter from 3539 to 4420. but in the following ten years the increase was less, by only 544 (12.3 per cent).

Date	Houses	Woods/Land	Cottages	Total
5.3.1861				1605.27
18.12.61				1650.77
7.8.62	1088.50	289.50	289.50	1667.50
23.2.63	1099.00	72.37	209.25	1380.62
30.9.63	1117.00	72.37	203.25	1392.62
25.8.64	2254.25	83.81	260.62	2598.68
10.10.65	2266.00	82.82	260.62	2609.44
9.10.66	2265.50	81.82	261.18	2608.50
3.8.68	2367.75	80.07	251.25	2699.07
26.1.70	2381.25	83.68	254.25	2719.18
1871*	2449.75	85.00	246.00	2780.75
25.3.72	2502.75	85.00	249.75	2837.50
21.5.73	2583.25	84.50	261.75	2929.50

* *The same amounts were returned twice, in March and August.*

It will be noted that the proportion of the total values accounted for by the housing section was 88.2 per cent in 1873, as against only 65.3 per cent in 1862, after the development of Haywards Heath had already begun. Presumably, this category presumably included all rateable property not classed as cottages.

Above, Hilton's later premises adjoining the playing fields at
Heathmere. Below, the showrooms built on the same
site in 1932. Demolished 1980.

Hilton's funeral office, next to the showroom.

Ardlin (perhaps originally Brunswick House), in The Broadway.
Latterly it housed a dentists' practice.

Ardlin, 1938-89, as the offices of the Haywards Heath Building Society.

Harry Plummer's office at Lyntonville, in Hazelgrove Road, after he became the Society's Secretary in 1897.

INTO THE 20TH CENTURY

B Y the time the Census was taken on 3 April 1881, Haywards Heath was well established. The growth of the town is shown by the development of its local government. In 1872 an urban sanitary authority responsible for public health was set up. Local tradesmen were well represented among its original members: they included two innkeepers, and a third joined them at the next election, besides a carman, Thomas Bannister and the Vicar. Meetings were held monthly at the Station Inn, and the offices were first in Perrymount Road, later in Boltro Road. In 1894 the sanitary authority was superseded by an urban district council. By 1871 there was already a police constable living in the cottages beside the Station Hotel, and by 1891 four officers, including a superintendent and a sergeant, were living in the police station established nearby in 1887; by 1907 three sergeants and 23 constables were stationed there. By 1938 there were a superintendent, a sergeant and two constables.

The London, Brighton and South Coast railway had always been one of the salient features of the town, although a tollgate-keeper was to be found in Wivelsfield Road as late as 1879; the old toll house was occupied as late as 1881 by a coachman and his family. At this time an extension of the station facilities was contemplated; a branch line to Horsted Keynes was constructed in the following year. By 1887 G Simmins and Gasson, a firm with offices in Crawley, East Grinstead and Horley, was conducting a weekly stock market at the station.

Dennis Warnett's shop still stood opposite the station entrance, but the butcher's shop had been taken over by Walter Marshall, a Wiltshire man already in his mid-forties. A few years later Warnett himself had departed: in 1887 Stephen Button was running the shop, and by 1891 Alfred Street, who described himself as a 'tea dealer and provision merchant', was there with his wife. The household at the butcher's shop next door was less straightforward: the Census return shows as its head Jane Pierce, a 50-year-old 'housekeeper', with a young nephew living with her who was the butcher's assistant. The butcher himself was merely lodging in the house with his family, perhaps in preparation to assuming control: he was a young man who evidently had come from Brighton only recently.

At 16 Boltro Road, next door to the wine merchant, stood the hairdressing establishment run by Frederick Whall, a Lindfield man aged 29; this was visited every market day by W E Kimber, a Lindfield tailor. Further up the road were Thomas Bannister's house, Limehurst, on the opposite side, and Ellensleigh, where Maxwelton House now stands, a house occupied by Walter Fry, a Devonshire man in business as a photographer in Brighton employing seven men and six women.

On the other side of the line, Frederick Beeny's 'noted stores for first-class grocery and provisions' and a wide range of other wares was flourishing on the corner of Mill Green Road. He was a Hailsham man, the son of Herbert Beeny, a grocer at Windmill Hill. He seems to have been well educated, and prospered early. In 1881, when he was only 28, his family contained three young children, and the household already included a nursemaid, a general servant, a milliner and shop assistants. In 1878 he had built a warehouse behind Fern House opposite. In 1891 the household included a Wiltshire girl who was the resident bookkeeper and other staff, and in 1894 he built stables for his delivery vehicles in Mill Green Road. He was to become increasingly active in the community, and served as a director of the building society from its earliest days, and as chairman for a period. His business survived until the 1930s. In Station Road was a shop run by Samuel Jerred, described as a grocer and bricklayer, and there was a tobacconist at 1 Oakfield Terrace in Perrymount Road.

A photograph of The Star and Clifton Terrace at The Broadway dated 1900 shows a terrace of four substantial residences next to the inn, with a couple of smaller houses beyond. Edward Watts had his chemist's shop on the corner, next to William Vincent's business; by 1887 he had been replaced by Thomas James Barnett, and he was followed a couple of years later by Richard Orchard Hayes, a 30-year-old man who remained there until shortly before the first World War.

Ardlin still stands on the opposite side of the road. In the 1950s the frontage of the house was drastically altered when the Haywards Heath Building Society moved into the building. At the turn of the century it was the home of Dr A H Newth, an Aberdeen graduate in medicine then practising as a general practitioner who had served as junior medical officer at the asylum. Dr Charles Neate also was practising in Sydney Road during the 1890s, and a dentist, John Glassington, was to be found in the road by the turn of the century. At that time another doctor, Patrick Griffith, was practising in Muster Green.

In July 1887 the Holy Cross home was opened in Bolnore Road, on the west of the town, by an Anglican community of sisters from Wapping; Elizabeth Neale, a sister of the hymnologist John Mason Neale, founded the community in 1857, and was Superior of the new house. It became St Stephen's orphanage and convalescent home, and in 1891 the community had 68 members as well as an assistant superior, with a gardener, laundry matron and their family in the lodge close by. A laundry was built in 1900, and further buildings were added in 1906-7. The sisters moved to Nottingham in 1979, and their buildings are now offices called Grosvenor Hall.

In 1897 the chapel of the Holy Spirit was opened on a site given by Dr T A Compton in Sydney Road. Services for men only were held there between 1902 and 1909. Then on 1 October 1916 it became the focal point of the new conventional district of St Richard to serve the needs of the northern part of the parish, and a house and garden were built. A parish room was provided in 1908 at the top of Paddockhall Road in premises now occupied by Colemans the solicitors, but this was closed when the conventional district was formed in October 1916.

In Asylum twitten (St John's Road) the chapel of the Ascension was opened in 1895, St Wilfrid's parish having absorbed Asylum Corner, at the southern end of Wivelsfield Road at Rocky Lane, during the previous year.

In New England Fields an iron mission church had been opened on 15 August 1882; it was enlarged with financial help from Miss Mary Otter, who was living at Chandos Lodge in Paddockhall Road by 1895. It reopened on 2 February 1886, and named as the Church of the Presentation after the festival celebrated on that day, but not until 15 August 1897 was a permanent church opened.

However, the road had yet to be constructed. As late as May 1890 the *Mid Sussex Times* reported, 'We learn that it is a positive fact that this road will now be made'. But a couple of months later there were no signs of activity, and the paper became impatient. By the end of the year it seems that the road had been completed, for John Piper, the grocer in South Road, had opened a shop there. Further signs of development were shown when the present church was opened in 1897, and the old building became the Sunday School.

At that time the Wesleyan Methodist mission was established nearby in Perrymount Road. In 1898 the superintendent minister at Lewes, the Reverend W L Bennett, was appointed to Haywards Heath with his manse in Sydney Road. Sunday and weekday meetings were held at first at Frederick Whall's hairdressing shop in Boltro Road; but the congregation soon outgrew this venue, and the meetings were transferred to Thomas Bannister's offices. The foundation stones of the present church were laid on 2 May 1900, and it was in use by the following August and opened formally in October, when Mr Bennett was succeeded by the Reverend Stephen Sullings. In 1912 the premises were extended with the erection of a temporary hut on permanent foundations; it was replaced only when the present Wesley hall opened in July 1959.

Public recreational facilities had already existed in the town for some years.

The Heath (Clair Meadow) nearby did not become a recreation ground until the Queen's golden jubilee in 1887; in 1900 a cricket pavilion was provided there. In 1897 the Urban District Council borrowed £3,000 in order to mark Her Majesty's diamond jubilee by acquiring Victoria Park for public use, and it imposed by-laws that met with some protest. In 1889 assembly rooms were built in Boltro Road. A public hall was provided in South Road near Sussex Square by private sponsors. In 1891 a gardener and his family were living there, presumably as caretakers, and the Conservative Association was to be found there in 1899. In June 1904 the hall was handed over to the Council on condition that a free reading room was provided.

There was also a parish house in Hazelgrove Road, known as The Institute; in 1891 it also was housing a gardener with his family and an elementary school teacher as lodger. The following year it became St Wilfrid's parish room, and French classes were held there.

The establishment run by Joshua Jones in The Broadway, later known as The Star hotel towards the end of the century, was a beer house in 1866, and continued as such until at least 1881. Another beer retailer active locally in the mid 1860s was Stephen Jones. He may have been a relation of Joshua, but we know nothing further of him. In addition to The Triangle (now The Heath) in Sussex Road, there was Charles Tester in the town in the early 1870s; he was probably a brother of Thomas Tester, of the Rose and Crown in Cuckfield at the same period. There was also Jesse Randall, who was selling beer in Wivelsfield Road during the late 1870s.

In 1887 Sharp and Sons are listed at The Brewery, probably at the junction of Mill Green and Queens Roads; but they seem to have existed for only a short time, as had Hamilton and Company in the late 1870s. Willoughby Power was a brewer in the town for a few years about 1880; his address was given as 1 Heather Cottages in Lewes Road. At the turn of the century John Dudney, Sons and Company were in business for several years, with stores in Perrymount Road.

Such enterprises as the Sergison Arms at the western end of Muster Green, also known as The Dolphin, the Station Hotel, the Burrell Arms or perhaps even the Liverpool Arms near the Coffee Tavern in Station Road were of a higher status. In these, the landlord was described as 'licensed victualler', 'innkeeper' or similarly. In the new century some at least were owned by breweries; in 1901 the Sussex Hotel had been taken over by the Southdown Brewery, and the Liverpool Arms was run by Nalder and Collyer by 1906.

In the Crossways (Sussex Square) area, the Sussex Hotel was in this category; like some of his fellows, the landlord, Jacob Grist, had additional employment, for he was also a farmer. No doubt the hotel's trade did not come from the

Sussex and Wivelsfield Roads, but relied more on trade from the more prosperous area north of the crossroads. But the number of public houses gave rise to some misgivings. In 1904 the Vicar, the Reverend T G Wyatt, wished their number to be reduced.

In 1885 Hazelgrove Park, which had stood empty for two years, was acquired for a community of Belgian canonesses. In the following July a group of the sisters settled in the mansion, and formed the nucleus of the community of sixty to eighty sisters to form the priory of Our Lady of Good Counsel that survived until the community moved to Sayers Common in 1978. The convent buildings now house a restaurant and a club.

The sisters arrived in July 1886, and set about adapting the house as a school for girls of the upper classes, who included the author Daisy Ashford. They added further conventual buildings at this time. In 1891 the community included six teachers offering instruction in history, piano, arithmetic, geography, French, English and needlecraft. There were also two sisters designated as sacristan and 'procurating' (housekeeper), five servants and nine boarding pupils. A Belgian priest was living in the lodge, together with a gardener and another housekeeper.

Clearly the Sussex Road area was not on the same social level as that north of Crossroads. In 1879 Mr Clarke's *Local directory* had noted only the Primitive Methodist chapel and the Congregational church as 'principal places of worship' in the area. But in that year the Zion Strict Baptist chapel was built in Sussex Road by William Knight, a horticulturist who lived at Jireh House, in fulfilment of a vow to do so if he prospered in business. He continued as its minister until the end of the century.

The Strict Baptists were already well established in the district. About 1865 George Wickham, a grocer in Danehill who was a member of the chapel there, started to hold services in a room at Scaynes Hill, and at the same period William Philpott, a former lay reader, held services in his own house at Burgess Hill, moving to Scaynes Hill within two or three years to continue Wickham's meetings at Awbrook Farm. When the farm was sold, a small chapel was built on the site. It was replaced by a fresh chapel, encouraged by the zeal of Mr Knight.

Petlands, the house near the junction of Hazelgrove Road and New England Road, provides another literary association with the town. For four years in the early 1850s it was the home of Isaac Sewell, the father of the author Anna Sewell, who is remembered for *Black Beauty*. He was a Quaker, described as a maltster, brewer and coal merchant at the time of the Census in 1851.

From the far end of New England Road runs America Lane. It takes its name from the agricultural colony set up in the 1820s by William Allen, the

Quaker philanthropist, to relieve the distress of impoverished agricultural labourers in Lindfield by encouraging self-sufficiency through the cultivation of an acre of land. Why the colony became known as the America colony is not clear. Very possibly it was because it was situated on the edge of the parish and away from the village community, so that paupers received in the colony may be said to have been 'sent to America', and became just as remote from the village as if they had been sent overseas; or perhaps because the enterprise engendered in the colony was reminiscent of the pioneering spirit among the American settlers.

An institution in Paddockhall Road that seems to have had a brief existence was St Christopher's convalescent home. This had been established about 1882 at Holly House, with twenty beds for the children of gentlemen of limited incomes. In April 1881 the house had been occupied merely by a caretaker and his family, and ten years later it was returned as unoccupied. The area from which the home took its patients is not clear; it was near the station, and perhaps it was established to serve Londoners. There was no adequate hospital in the area for another 25 years; a minute of the Congregational church meeting in January 1888 records that the pastor proposed that a collection be made for the Sussex County Hospital in Brighton 'as several members of the church had been receiving benefits therefrom'. By this time the convalescent home had already disappeared. But a couple of years later a District Nurses Fund was started. This continued until the County Council undertook the provision of the service in 1911.

An indication of developing culture in the town is provided by the early appearance of a pianoforte dealer, James Ford. In 1903 he planned a music warehouse in the Boltro Road. This probably was near Heath Square; but in 1907 his address is given as Market Place. This perhaps is a mistake, but evidently his business had prospered, for at that time John James Ford is shown as living at Blantyre in Perrymount Road, the address listed for the business in 1915, when it seems that he had quit Boltro Road.

Booksellers also had made their appearance. In 1879 W L Hinwood was to be found at 4 Liverpool Cottages in Sydney Road; he became the manager of W H Smith's bookstall when it was set up at the railway station around 1890. In 1887 the firm of Robinson and Plummer, printers, bookbinders and stationers, set up in South Road, and in 1890 John Morton Robinson was in business as a secondhand bookseller and printer, also in South Road. At the end of the century Miss Annie Robinson was a stationer and bookseller, probably continuing the same business; she retired in 1938.

There was also a stationer at the top of Sussex Road at Crossroads: Rhoda Edwards, the wife of a hairdresser, John Edwards, was so described in 1891.

The previous year the shop had become a sub post office. An indication that trade was prospering in this part of the town by the 1890s was given by the *Mid Sussex Times* reporting, in February 1890, that there were two watchmakers 'where but a short time ago one could not find a living'. A little later the paper noted that some preliminary work for laying pavements had started at Triangle Road, and in 1899 there was a poultry feed maker in Gower Road.

The Edwards family remained until at least 1895, but by the end of the century Miss Priscilla Chinnock had taken over. There was another office further down the road; this was run by William Gater, a stationer and cabinet maker who lived at Kentville Cottage in Wivelsfield Road, and he continued until the first World War.

The main post office had moved to Boltro Road after John Meux's death. In the early 1890s it was run by John Samuel at The Yews, previously a private house, before the buildings behind the police station were built in 1894. This area was already developing; in 1890 the extension of the 'up' platform at the station was seen as an 'index of increased business'. Job Norton, a tailor and outfitter 'from Oxford Street, W.', established himself at Number 4 near the police station, and Frederick Whall was selling cricket equipment and tennis balls. By 1913 his business had been taken over by his son Percy, and Frederick, another member of the family, had set up there as an optician.

A firm of manufacturing chemists was active in Paddockhall Road at this period. In 1895 Cripps and Edwards were listed with an address at The Laboratory; the principal was Richard Cripps, who was described as an analytical and consulting chemist. He was still there in 1899 and probably in 1907, as plans were made for an extension to the premises towards the end of that year. But *Kelly's Directory* no longer listed him there. In 1915 the firm is shown in Brighton.

A tradesman whose business survived until recent years was Thomas Hever, a fishmonger with a shop next door to the Burrell Arms at Commercial Square. The business originated in Cuckfield about 1880, and moved to Haywards Heath in the late 1880s. In 1891 his family included Frederick Ellmer, his brother-in-law, who was working with him in the shop. Hever seems to have disappeared by 1895, and the business continued as Ellmer Brothers. It finally closed in 1984.

Other businesses appeared in the town at this period. Some we have already mentioned, and others seem to have survived for a short period only. In 1882 Prior and Company were 'cream separators' at Bridgers mill, although, as we have noted, the firm of Jenner and Higgs controlled the mill; in 1881 Samuel Jenner and Caleb Higgs, described as millers and corn merchants, were living in Sydney Road. In 1890 the mill was owned by the firm of G W Bailey and

Son. Ellis Turner was in business as a florist at Mill House, Balcombe Road, in 1899. At this time Anne Hayllar had her toyshop in Hazelgrove Road near Crossroads; later she became a 'wardrobe dealer'.

Another feature of the town's development was the increasing number of people offering apartments. These sprung up in different parts of the town: even in 1899 they were to be found in New England Road, Sydney Road, Oathall Road and even Muster Green. By 1907 the number of apartments had increased dramatically. It seems clear that there was a demand for what is now called 'social housing'. *The Mid Sussex Times* had commented on the rapid growth in housing. 'At Lucastes there would be a hundred or two hundred houses built, and in Petlands Wood they were making roads for about the same number of houses'.

A number of tradesmen lived above the shop, but others lived at a distance from their place of work. In 1891 staff at the asylum were distributed over an area that stretched from Triangle Road and Hazelgrove Road to Haywards Road; railway personnel were living in New England Road and Sussex Road; and one postman was lodging in Franklynn Road, while another was living in Triangle Road. In February 1897 the *Mid Sussex Times* expressed uneasiness at the cost of providing social housing at a time of economic difficulty.

Colemans' offices in Paddockhall Road near Boltro Chambers.
The former parish room is on the left.

70

Above, The Broadway from Muster Green. Undated photograph.
Below, the same, facing Muster Green. Undated photograph.

Above, the chemist's shop when occupied by R O Hayes.
Below, the same shop as it is today. The name Dixon's
(for W H Dixon) is still to be seen at the entrance.

Appendix: Some Early Tradesmen

Charles Clarke, printer and bookbinder

It is claimed that Charles Clarke founded his business in 1871 at premises in Boltro Road, but when the Census was taken on 2 April there was no trace either of him or of his house, and it would seem that his business was started much later in the year. The earliest known example of his output is his *Local directory and year book* of 1879, and a couple of years later he published the first issue of the *Mid Sussex Times*, the local paper that is still published from the same premises.

He was born in Bideford, Devon, in 1841, and was apprenticed to a printer and bookbinder at the age of 14. During his apprenticeship his master founded a newspaper, and the young Clarke was introduced to journalism. Later he migrated to Cornwall and thence to Somerset. In 1864 he came to work in Uckfield, and lived in Fletching. There he married his first wife, who died in November 1907, and his three eldest surviving children were born. From thence he came to Haywards Heath.

The Census in 1881 records his family at their home, 7 Boltro Road. The eldest of his children was his daughter Mary Ann, who was aged 13 at the time. Four years earlier she had laid a memorial stone at the Primitive Methodist chapel; his involvement in church affairs is noticed on pages 52 and 53. His twin sons, George and James, later joined him in his business. He died in March 1921.

George Hilton, cabinet maker and furniture dealer

About 1880 George Hilton arrived in Haywards Heath from Hastings with a bag of tools, and set up in business at Crossways (Sussex Square). By the mid 1880s he was at Acton House, South Road. In due course he became a local councillor and a Justice of the Peace, and he was chairman of the Urban District Council by the time of the first World War.

He was a man of strong principles, and disapproved of smoking and Sunday games. He and his family were staunch supporters of the Primitive Methodist church, as described on pages 53 and 54, and in 1909 he was president of the Mid Sussex Evangelical Free Church Council.

He had a sincere concern for his fellows. He strongly supported the plan for a cottage hospital when it was put before the Urban District Council early in 1906, and he was one of only two councillors who recommended its support from the rates, against the prevailing view that such action would discourage the voluntary contributions on which the hospital was to rely. He was also a manager of the council school for many years, and supported its development. He died shortly before the second World War.

William Andrew (or St Andrew) Vincent, watch and clock maker, jeweller

William Andrew Vincent was born in Bolney, apparently the eldest surviving child of William Vincent, a Bolney man described as a builder, and perhaps the grandson of the Reverend William Vincent, whose address was given in 1839 as St Andrews, Bolney.

The family do not appear in Haywards Heath earlier than 1878. William Andrew is listed in the successive editions of *Kelly's directory* as running a 'fancy repository' in addition to being a watchmaker, and in Clarke's *Local directory* for 1879 he is described as 'watchmaker, jeweller and fancy repository, Clifton Place, North Road', but his displayed advertisement there gives greater prominence to his work as a 'watch & clock maker, jeweller and silversmith'. His advertisement in the first issue of the *Mid Sussex Times* on 12 January 1881 elaborated on this information: 'Berlin Wool and Fancy Repository. Agent for P. and P. Campbell, the Perth Dyers'.

Clifton Place ran north from The Star inn at The Broadway. There was a chemist's shop in the parade by 1871, and it seems to have been developing as a commercial centre in the new town.

His wife, Mary, died on 26 December 1880 at the age of 26. In 1881, when he was aged 30, his premises are described as a 'watchmaker's shop', and his household included only one boarder. However, his father was also living on the premises with the rest of the family. Probably his sister Ida Ann, a girl of 15, was helping him in the shop, for she is described as a shop assistant.

By 1887 he seems to have given up business, for *Kelly's directory* has no entry for him, listing only 'Vincent, Mrs, fancy repository, Perrymount Road'. The business had been taken over by his mother (or stepmother), for in 1899 her name appears as Ruth Vincent, the same as that of his father William's wife in both the relevant Census returns.

But William Andrew was still active, although no longer working on his own behalf. He was on the original committee of the Haywards Heath Horticultural Society, founded in 1889. At the time of the 1891 Census he is still living at 2 Clifton Place, but as a member of his father's family; the father is then described as 'clerk of works', aged 72.

Early in the present century, presumably after his mother's death, the family seems to have dispersed. By 1912 he was in business again on his own, still describing himself as merely 'watchmaker and jeweller'. At that time he had two addresses at the eastern, less prosperous, end of the town: Gower Road and Posbrook in Ashenground Road. But between 1913 and 1917 he is shown with one address only: Victoria Watch and Clock Works, Sussex Square. It may be that the works might have been situated in the basement of Victoria House, which stood just to the south of the square, on the corner of Gower Road.

It is worth noting that in 1915 *Kelly's Directory* gave his occupation merely as 'watchmaker', and therefore clocks would seem to have played a minor part in his business. But by 1922 he had retired, and thenceforth he is listed without an occupational designation and with his address at Posbrook. In 1927 his name disappeared from the directories.

Jesse Finch, builder

Jesse Finch was born about 1843. He left school when aged nine, and was taught bricklaying by his father. He came from West Hoathly, and set up his own business about 1866; by 1871, when he was living at 2 Finches Cottages in Sydney Road, he was employing four men. Eventually he moved to the site of the later bus station in Perrymount Road, and gradually the range of his activities was extended to include an insurance agency and an undertaking business. He became one of the most prominent tradesmen in the town, having also taken over a well established business in Balcombe. Like many other prominent tradesmen, he served as chairman of the Haywards Heath Building Society, and he sat on the Urban District Council.

In 1906 his business was taken over by his son Horace, then aged about 40.

Herbert Brown and the South Road Coach Works

Towards the eastern end of South Road, behind the parade on the south now occupied by Boots and Budgens, used to stand a long-established garage. The western wall of the earlier building had a sign bearing the words 'South Road Coach Works'.

The business was started by Alfred James Isted, who was working in Franklynn Road as a carriage builder and wheelwright in 1907. By 1915 he had moved his business into South Road, where Herbert Brown, who lived at 5 Gower Road, also had set up in business as a cycle agent.

In the early 1920s Mr Brown took the business over from Mr Isted, although in 1924 both men were listed as motor engineers in South Road, Mr Brown's business being listed as a company. At this period Mr Brown was serving also in the town's fire brigade. At first the workshop stood near Canton Cottage where now stands Lloyds Bank at the top of Haywards Road, and only later was it moved near Sussex Square.

In 1979 the business was transferred to the former Golding's garage in Market Place by the then owner, Mr Brown's son-in-law Fred Fairhall. He entered into partnership with the then Golding's manager, Chris Jones, who controls the business today.

Arthur Harold Langridge, builder

Arthur Langridge began his working life under his uncle, Jesse Finch. From 1908 he was a member of the Wesleyan Methodist church in Perrymount Road, with an especial interest in young people. He ran a very successful Sunday school, and he was a devoted supporter of the church, both financially and actively.

During the first World War it was noticed that his hearing was defective, but that did not hamper him. He lost some fingers on one hand as the result of an accident while he was working, and he set up his own business with the compensation he received. He lived at Weybridge in Eastern Road.

He died on 27 May 1979.

Herbert Brown's early premises near Haywards Road.

Above, Brown's garage – entrance to A J Isted's coach works,
before the first World War. The mural sign was still visible until the
building occupied by Boots was built. Below, the works in early days.

The entrance to the garage as it was in the 1950s or 1960s.

THE EDWARDIAN ERA

K ING Edward VII came to the throne in January 1901. The period saw living standards, job security and standards of health rise among the lower classes. Early in the century, one writer commented that the town's appearance was 'in keeping with that of the well-groomed man of wealth'. His comments are obviously biased, and perhaps influenced by the number of large houses in the town.

The suggestion of prosperity is supported by his remark that 'the town is well paved, and admirably lighted with incandescent gas'. The *Mid Sussex Times* reported in 1898 that land was available for housing development in Ashenground, Haywards and Heath Roads, and the Haywards Heath Building Society helped householders with mortgages in Haywards Road in the period before 1914, but Gower and Western Roads were even more favoured.

However, the auctioneer Scott Pitcher did not succeed in securing a very substantial mortgage of £1,000 in 1902 on a house and land in Lucastes Avenue, although he became a director of the society in the following year. In July 1913 49 acres of building land in the Lucastes estate was put up for sale; the title to the land was traced from the will of Jacob Caffyn in 1850. At that date Winnals and Lincoln Lodge were already standing at the junction of Lucastes Avenue and Paddockhall Road, and to the west stood Lucastes, Lucas Grange and The Mount. The eastern end of Lucastes Road was fairly densely developed on its northern side, but there seems to have been little development elsewhere in the area, of which the land included in the sale was only a part. Bluntswood Road was merely a right of way.

The availability of health insurance was increasing at this period, and was to be extended under the National Insurance Act of 1911. The provision of hospital facilities generally was increasing. A Miss Eliot, a former nurse who lived at Asylum Corner, died in 1904, and left £600 in her will to set up a hospital either in the town or in Wivelsfield, the parish in which she lived. With the support of local doctors, but notwithstanding the reluctance of the Urban District Council to give needed financial support, the Eliot Cottage Hospital was established in 1906 at Eliot House, a semi-detached house rented for three years in Ashenground Road, with Mary Barrett as matron. The *Mid Sussex Times* reported on 7 January 1908 that it had five patients. Subsequently the other house of the pair was acquired.

Plans for a new building were approved in March 1911, and in the following year the hospital was moved to land acquired from Sir James Bradford and Captain Warden Sergison in Butlers Green Road, and renamed the King Edward VII Eliot Memorial Hospital. It had accommodation for twelve patients, and was maintained by voluntary subscriptions, with a management committee appointed by the subscribers. In 1915 22 patients could be admitted, and a recreation room was provided behind the buildings. A new wing was added in 1916, and a mortuary and X-Ray room were provided in 1918. A nurses' home was built at the hospital in 1926, and a chapel was added in 1928, designed by the architect J L Cooper. Other facilities were added between 1920 and 1963.

The almshouses established by Sir James Bradford nearby had been opened in 1911. In 1917 a cemetery had been opened in Western Road, and part was consecrated by the Bishop of Chichester on 6 June for use by churchpeople; St Wilfrid's churchyard was closed a year later.

Towards the end of the nineteenth century the Haywards Heath Building Society had been granting mortgages on properties in the less prosperous south of the town; by 1914 a total of 75 mortgages had been taken out on properties to such folk as bricklayers and the owner of an unsuccessful small laundry in Franklynn Road. Builders and other speculators such as tradesmen and publicans also took out mortgages with the society. Gower Road and Western Road were the most popular roads, each attracting 15 mortgages at this period. No less than 11 mortgages were taken out in 1898 on houses in this area. At the other end of the town, around the station, the pattern was much the same; Queens Road attracted 8 mortgages in the period from 1902, and speculators had planned 22 houses for the road and a pair each of cottages and houses in Church Avenue; more prosperous Sydney Road attracted only 4 mortgages.

There were early signs of increasing business activity near the station. In Boltro Road E C Baldwin proposed to build two houses with shops in 1901, and Charles Ballard was to be found there in 1907. Larger businesses were also beginning to appear. In 1905 Thomas Other Windsor, with an address at Invermay, Lucastes Avenue, was described as manufacturer of Thermogene, a form of medicated wadding. By 1907 his company had a manager, Harry Vivash, and by 1913 it had moved to premises in Queens Road now occupied by the agricultural equipment dealers E O Culverwell. The factory was extended in 1919 and in the 1930s. The Liverpool Arms had been taken over by the brewers Nalder and Collyer by 1906, and by 1901 the Sussex Hotel was owned by the Southdown Brewery.

Early in the century the Haywards Heath and District Sanitary Steam Laundry was be found near the junction of Sydney Road and Oathall Road in buildings that still survive, and another laundry in 1902 had been started by R Stoner in Gower Road. Barclays Bank had a branch in the Market Place under a manager by 1907; previously its business had been dealt with by the solicitor Edward Waugh as agent from his office in Boltro Road. By 1913 both the Joint Water Board and the Electric Light and Power Company were also to be found in Boltro Road, as were the architect Arthur Pannett and the auctioneer Scott Pitcher, who was close to Thomas Bannister's yard in the Market Place. The South of England Dairies had opened a shop in Perrymount Road in 1902, and soon needed to extend them.

The motor and cycle dealer C W Wood was active in building developments in the area at that time, and Ben F Stott, draper and milliner who was prominent enough to proclaim his business activities on the side of the first omnibus in the town, was planning extensions to his premises in 1905. The business centre of South Road attracted only five mortgages during this period to 1914, although there was a good deal of business development. In 1902 Henry Uridge planned to extend his house and shop near Crossroads, and Mrs M Watts, a fruiterer, needed stabling, as did Percy Rowland, the fishmonger. George Hilton need a new warehouse in 1912, and in 1913 a boot repairer, T M Verrall, needed a temporary shed and a fresh cottage at the rear of his shop.

The Co-Operative Stores had appeared at the junction of Gower Road with Sussex Road in the mid-1890s. Their plans for extending their premises give additional evidence that business in the town was prospering. A bakehouse and housing for carts were needed in 1904, and a garage in 1913, when a shed was placed at the rear of the shop, which had been extended in 1908.

There were facilities for public recreation at this time. Entertainments were staged at the public hall as early as 1902 by the amateur dramatic society, which was supported by some of the most prominent families in the town. We learn from a playbill for a show on 15-16 April that there were two categories of seats: 'first seats' (presumably those nearest the stage) were twice the price of 'second seats'. In 1904 a reading room was opened at the Constitutional Club in South Road, and a public reading room at the public hall. A 'picture theatre', known as the Heath Theatre, was in The Broadway by 1912. The site is still marked by a turret on the roof. Children were charged two pence for admission, and a Miss Hatton used to accompany the silent films on the piano. The Church Lads Brigade had its premises in Gower Road, and its drill hall and billiard room were let out.

At this period there was a men's society known as the Haywards Heath Brotherhood. This was an interdenominational initiative designed to attract men from outside the church congregations. There was a Brotherhood band, and by 1914 those over 14 years of age were admitted. The Brotherhood met on Sundays in Sussex Road, and held lectures at the Wesleyan Methodist church in Perrymount Road; other meetings were held at the Congregational church in Wivelsfield Road.

The Pleasant Sunday Afternoon meetings were also popular. The surviving records relate to the period 1908-15. No less than 61 people are shown as attending during 1908. These included W T Fowle, a jeweller in the Broadway, George Langridge, a carpenter, and W H Tolhurst, who became head gardener to Sir Alexander Kleinwort at Bolnore. In 1909 the group was joined, amongst others, by R Jury, who ran a hardware shop in South Road, and Walter Yeandle, who worked as a printer for Charles Clarke. Another tradesman in South Road, a boot repairer named Thomas Verrall, also joined in, as did F Dudney, the landlord of the Burrell Arms. These meetings were organized by the churches, and were intended to be non-denominational. But the meetings seem to have had an especial appeal to nonconformists.

Relations between the churches appear to have been cordial. Thomas Heywood, the minister of the Primitive Methodist church in Sussex Road in 1907 until he moved to London for health reasons, seems to have been readily accepted by his colleagues in other churches, and was a close friend of the chaplain at the Priory nearby.

In 1910 the patronage of the living of St Wilfrid's was taken over by the Bishop of Chichester from the Vicar of Cuckfield, and the following year the parish was extended to include College Road and Balcombe Road.

Sussex Road in 1904.

Wivelsfield Road in 1911.

Sussex Square as troops were marching to the front in 1914.

South Road. An undated photograph taken during the War by
Harry Tullett, a photographer active in the road during
the early years of the century.

BETWEEN THE WARS

THE period between the two World Wars was marked by social unrest and economic depression following the relaxation of social attitudes in the earlier years of the century. But the town seemed little affected by these disturbances. There were still plenty of people who raised mortgages on property in the town. In the period 1919 to 1929 the greatest number of mortgages were taken out in the less prosperous areas of the town, away from the principal roads: Sydney, Queens and Gordon Roads in the northern area of the town; and the *Mid Sussex Times* reported in 1928 that Gordon Road had been repaired with material from the Brighton Aquarium. Gower, Western, Sussex and New England Roads to the south also attracted numbers of mortgagors. Bents Wood was developed in the 1930s, and during the 1920s and more especially 1930s fresh roads were constructed in the areas around Ashenground, Franklynn and Wivelsfield Roads, and the area around Oathall Avenue.

Substantial house building also was taking place in Park Road, Wood Ride, Gander Hill and the Petlands and Lucastes estates. Many premises in the Broadway and South Road also were extended, and additions were made to St Helena's convalescent home in 1924. By 1938 The Oaks nursing home had appeared in Paddockhall Road.

Many individuals and organizations were responsible for planning these developments. The builders W Elliott Stedman in Boltro Road and especially Arthur Langridge, the architects S H Tiltman of Brighton and H G Turner in Boltro Chambers, the sanitary engineer F T Hackman in the Broadway, the indefatigable Harry Plummer, secretary of the Haywards Heath Building Society, Arthur Purvey, who seems to have been a retired builder, and K G Holman were prominent.

New England Road gained a parish room in 1919, and there was a sub-post office there by 1924. By that time post offices were to be found also at the corner of Mill Green and College Roads (run by Arthur H Bailey, perhaps related to the family a short distance away at the mill) as well as in South Road and Sussex Road. On 24 June 1917 the parish room beside the police station in Paddockhall Road became the office of a solicitor named George Coleman, who previously had been practising from Highlands House in Church Road.

The town already had a fire brigade in the 1890s, when the captain was a builder named Samuel Jerred, who was to be found at Yew Cottage, Sydney

Road. By 1904 George Clarke had become the captain with a team of ten men, and the fire station was in South Road, on the edge of Victoria Park. By the mid 1920s Herbert Brown had become the captain, and he remained in charge until the second World War. The South Road fire station was demolished in the 1980s.

A sign of prosperity elsewhere in the town and of the pervasive influence of the motor car is the number of garages built in this period. One of the earliest was planned in 1919 by Mr J V Taylor at Vinings in Church Road. Beeny's Stores followed in 1926 with one in Queens Road, only about four years before it was to become the Forrest Stores, and amongst others three were built for local clergy in 1927-8 and one for the Priory in 1932. Herbert Brown had taken over the South Road Coach Works by the early 1920s, and the Sergison Arms boasted a garage by 1924.

A little later the Dinnage family arrived from Uckfield. In 1925 Mrs J Dinnage, with an address at The Kellows, Sussex Road, set up in business with a shopfront and workshop, and extended her premises in 1928; presumably this was the cycle agency at 81-3 South Road that Mrs A D E Dinnage was running in 1938. Another member of the family was Leonard Dinnage, who lived in Queen's Road and was a partner in Broadley's, the men's outfitters next to Ardlin in the Broadway.

In 1934 J W Dinnage, Leonard's brother, who had been running a garage in Uckfield, leased a showroom and workshops from F B Walton as Dinnage's Garages Limited, and ceased his business activities in Uckfield. In the following years he installed two electric petrol pumps and extended his premises in Wivelsfield Road, where the business still thrives. The adoption of the old Congregational church as an Anglican church dedicated to St Edmund suggests that the community in this part of the town was prospering at this period.

During the 1920s and 1930s the town expanded rapidly. In 1921 the London and South Coast and associated railways were amalgamated to form the Southern Railway. The station was rebuilt in 1932, and in 1935 the lines to Brighton and Hastings were electrified.

In 1933 the International Rotary Club recognized the need for social housing to meet the needs of the unemployment caused by the recession. A company was formed in order to buy Franklands Wood for a housing society. In 1935 a block of flats was built in Reed Pond Walk, and by the time the second World War broke out about 280 houses had been completed. Brighton Borough Council also provided additional accommodation for staff at the mental hospital (later St Francis Hospital) with cottages off Kents Road and in Asylum Road (now Colwell Road).

There were other signs of trading confidence during the late 1920s. In New

England Road George Abbott set up his shop at no. 78, The White House, and G A Randall established his fruiterer's shop and sub-post office at 64. In Queens Road Ebenezer Wood set up as a cycle agent at 42-4. In 1938 all three enterprises were still flourishing.

Mushroom culture was planned for Lewes Road in 1936. No trace of this enterprise seems to have survived; but Frederick Slack, who had planned it, was living at St Mawes in Summerhill Lane. In 1937 the market gardeners H and G H Chapman built glasshouses on Paddockhall Gardens, now Nursery Close. There was also a small firm, The Pompeian, near the Thermogene building, that made beauty preparations.

A little earlier the three shops still surviving opposite The Star inn on Muster Green were built on a part of the garden at Clevelands by Miss E Cole, who owned the house, and in Clifton Terrace at this period was Rixon's store. This survived until the late 1970s, and extended to two shops, one a greengrocer's and the other a fishmonger's. There were three fishmongers in the town at this period: Macfisheries was the first to close, followed by Rixon's. The third, Ellmer's, survived until 1984. On the opposite side of the road Kenneth Lincoln, of Roger's Farm, Wivelsfield, established his pork butcher's shop, which survived until the late 1980s.

Larger tradesmen also were prospering. Hilton and Sons built a furniture depository in Hazelgrove Road, on the site now occupied by Fads, in the early 1920s, and in the early 1930s the firm built fresh premises on the site they already occupied in South Road, now part of The Orchards arcade. Another furnishing trader, Ernest Miller, built a showroom in The Broadway in the mid-1920s.

There were signs of increased church activity at this period. The town's civil parish was formed on 22 July 1934. At St Richard's church the facilities were extended between 1923 and 1928 to include a boys' club; when the present church was opened in 1938, the club was installed in the old church building. St Richard's parish was formed on 14 March 1939. In 1938 Elfinsward was made over to the diocese of Chichester as a conference centre by Mrs Gerald Moor. St Paul's Roman Catholic church was built in Hazelgrove Road between 1928 (when the foundation stone was laid) and 1930; a presbytery was added in 1935, and the Priory was extended between 1929 and 1934. In 1936 the Evangelical Free Church built a temporary hall in New England Road. There was a gospel hall in Franklynn Road by 1936, on a site opposite the present Franklynn Garage, and a hall in Eastern Road.

Changes were taking place also in the council schools. In 1933 the school in South Road became a senior school, still under Owen Freestone, who retired in 1937, and the juniors were transferred amicably to St Wilfrid's.

In October 1938 a large council senior school was opened on land that had already been acquired by the County Council in Oathall park, and became a school for 480 pupils of both sexes. It boasted a canteen, a library and a school choir. Several pupils went on to grammar school or technical college. In September 1939 about 180 children from London schools were evacuated, and came to share the premises while retaining their separate identity.

On 13 September 1932 the Broadway cinema was opened. It closed in 1954, and the building became J W Upton's furniture showroom. This closed in 1986, and the building was demolished in 1987 to be replaced by Capital House. The Perrymount Cinema near Commercial Square followed on 30 May 1936, and the building incorporated a dance hall and a restaurant. In its turn it closed in August 1972, and the building was demolished in 1984.

By 1938 there were a chain library and two banks, the Midland and the National Provincial, in The Broadway, and a branch of the Westminster Bank had been established on Muster Green. In Church Road a recreation room was built at the rear of Sharrow school in the summer of 1933, and a gymnasium followed on the same site in 1937. Both probably were built by Gilbert Kent, who undertook work for the school, and these buildings may have been part of the school premises, although this is not clear.

In 1933 Oaklands, the former home of Harry Treacher and of Sir James Bradford before his death in 1930, became the offices of the Urban District Council, the year before it merged with Cuckfield to form the Cuckfield Urban District Council. The East Sussex County Council established a clinic nearby in 1936.

Further commercialization of the area by 1935 is shown by the conversion of Hayes Barton in Boltro Road from a private house into professional offices for a firm of chartered accountants, Russell and Fleming. The building later became Barton Chambers, and is now Maxwelton House. Other professional firms were also to be found in the road; the solicitors Waugh and Company were well established, as were Houseman and Company.

Boltro Road, offices of Waugh
and Company, solicitors,
demolished 1991

Boltro Road Post Office,
demolished 1994

3 Perrymount Road. Offices of Bradley and Vaughan, estate agents,
now demolished, formerly the lodge for St Clair.

SCHOOLS

IN 1856, before St Wilfrid's parish church was built, a National elementary school was established in premises now occupied by the Christian Scientists in Church Road. It was supervised by the Reverend R E Wyatt, then a curate in Cuckfield who was to become the first vicar of the new parish. Early in the present century the school had eight assistant teachers and a capacity for 400 children with an average attendance of 369; but at the end of 1903 the then Vicar, the Rev T G Wyatt, complained in a letter to the *Mid Sussex Times* that the National school in the town had on its roll 68 children from Wivelsfield, 13 from Cuckfield and 4 from Keymer. At this time military discipline was taught at some schools, and from 1906 boys at the school were taught rifle shooting. This was continued for some years.

A new infants' school was opened in June 1895 by Archdeacon Sutton next to the existing school in Church Road to cater for 240 children. It had been financed by the Misses Otter. It had been designed by J Kennard and built by Thomas White, and boasted a playroom in the basement and three classrooms. In 1907 there were three assistant teachers and an average attendance of 167, and by 1915 the establishment had been increased to five teachers.

The 1902 Education Act replaced the multitude of school boards with local education authorities controlled by the Board of Education; it enjoined that religious instruction should be without denominational bias. The Board refused permission to build another church school in the north of the parish in 1904, and a Council mixed elementary school was established at Heathmere in South Road under Owen Freestone, formerly an assistant at the National school, who remained as head until his retirement in 1937. In 1907 the school moved to larger premises in an adjacent field, and by 1915 it was catering for 390 pupils.

By 1907 further council schools had appeared in the area. Heathmere had been shared with a pupil teachers' centre which complemented the teaching practice prescribed for young intending teachers with a secondary education of a high standard, and this centre occupied the entire house from 3 September 1907. The centre catered for about 100 girls; their training included religious knowledge from 20 May 1908.

Eventually the centre was replaced by the County secondary school for girls. An early headmistress was Lilian Vobes, a recent graduate of the

University of Wales; she was described by one of her pupils, Edith Quinn, who herself became a council teacher, as 'a brilliant woman [who] ruled by fear'. She was succeeded in 1913 by Annie Stevens, a Lindfield woman of the same age who had trained at Stockwell training college in London. The school was merged with Hove girls' grammar school about 1935, and Miss Stevens left the service of the local authority to establish her own girls' school at St Clair, a house near Commercial Square, which had been a gentleman's residence from at least 1870. A garage was added as late as 1930. In 1946 Miss Stevens sold the school to Mrs Joyce Grove and Miss F H Finlayson; in 1967 the household included Henry L Grove, who was commuting to London. The school closed in 1969, and the house was demolished in 1973.

There had been schools at the Priory and at the Holy Cross convent in Bolnore Road at the end of the nineteenth century, and in 1911 the Roman Catholic presence was increased when a school was opened in Haywards Road by St Joseph's convent of Kemp Town, Brighton. Temporary classrooms were erected by the school in 1918 and 1929, and an army hut was converted into a gymnasium in 1921. St Paul's school was opened in Oathall Road in the 1930s, and a primary school was attached to the church in Hazelgrove Road.

From the earliest years there had been also private educational facilities in the town. But some seem to have been short-lived. In 1866 *Kelly's directory* noted an 'academy' run by Dr Robert Henry Williams, who had recently arrived in the town. This must have been a very select establishment; in 1871 Dr Williams claimed to be a 'professor of analytical chemistry' and a 'lecturer in chemistry and natural philosophy'. He was living with his family and an older couple of independent means at Brunswick House, which stood beside The Star inn in Clifton Terrace. But he had disappeared by 1878. By 1882 Mary Upton, a dressmaker in her thirties, had replaced him, and she was joined by her sister Eliza by 1891.

Other schools were more modest affairs. Sarah Anna Pace was running a day school as early as 1845 at Chasemore House, Cuckfield. Later she called her establishment a 'ladies school': the 1871 Census gives her age as 65 and her address as 1 Portland Place, New (Boltro) Road, where evidently she had a family of lodgers, two of whom seem to have done the housework. In 1881, after she had retired, she was still living with lodgers at 3 Boltro Road. Other schools moved to fresh premises. By 1887 Miss Ellen Matthews had set up her school for young ladies at Coombe House, South Road, but in the early 1890s Miss Emma Matthews replaced this with a similar establishment at Sunnycroft, Oathall Road.

Many of these schools seem to have had a short life, perhaps succumbing to financial difficulties. One such was the small school run by a widow named

Isabella White, at 1 Heathfield Villas in Sydney Road. At the time of the 1881 Census she was catering for eight pupils that included her own children; but this seems to have been a very temporary affair, and probably was badly run. The following year Mrs White was listed as a private resident only in *Kelly's directory*.

Another similar institution was the boarding school for boys established at Petlands by a Scotswoman named Cecilia Blake before 1880. In 1881 there were twelve pupils, including Mrs Blake's own son; but by the following year the house had reverted to a private residence. At the same period Miss Elizabeth Mary Verrall was running what was called a 'ladies' school' at 1 Bourne House, Sussex Road. An auctioneer named Charles Verrall was to be found at the same address, so very probably the two were closely related.

Alfred Willmot also was attracted to private schoolteaching. He had been at St Wilfrid's school since 1865. Evidently that he had been a good disciplinarian, and his work had been praised by the school inspectors. However in 1882 the inspectors' comments became more critical. He seems to have suffered from ill-health, and was replaced by W J Davies.

But in 1890 he is shown as running a private boys' school at St Hilda'a Cottages in South Road, and as secretary of the Haywards Heath Horticultural Society; the following Census shows that his wife was actively involved with his school. Evidently the school was not a success, for it had ceased to exist before the end of the century, and by 1895 his control of the horticultural society had ended. He was still living at St Hilda's Cottages, but at the end of the century his address is given as Edelweiss in South Road, and he died in 1901. However his wife retained an interest in their former home; as late as 1912 the Plymouth Brethren were meeting in 'Mrs Willmot's room at St Hilda's villas, next to Victoria Park'.

Another school nearby was at Heathmere, opposite the top of Haywards Road. The house had been occupied by Thomas Gower, a brick manufacturer, who had secured the house in 1860 under the Enclosure award, and was still living there alone as an elderly widower with two servants on Census night in 1881. By 1890 it had become a boys' preparatory school run by Henry Soulser, a man of Swiss origin who seems to have settled in the town with other members of his family in Oathall Road. Philip Grandin, a man in his 30s, was joint head. In 1891 they had twelve boarders, together with a resident cook and housemaid. By 1895 the school had been taken over by Charles Rainsford Draper; he was still there in 1899, and he died in 1905.

The house was offered for sale on 5 June 1901, when it was owned by Edward Danvers Draper and claimed to be 'now used as a school for young gentlemen, for which it is admirably adapted'. The accommodation therefore gives us an idea of the arrangements to be found in a private school at this period. The house had six bedrooms with a bathroom and linen cupboard on the first floor and four further bedrooms on the top floor, all with high ceilings. The bathroom was described as having a 'housemaid's sink' for the ablutions of the domestic staff. Below there was a study and a water closet, with further lavatories and three cellars in the basement. The kitchen, with a scullery, larder and further toilet facilities, was on the ground floor, together with one class room, a large dining room and a smaller drawing room. There were also some stabling and a tennis court.

On that occasion the house failed to find a buyer. Heathmere school continued at Hillcrest in Heath Road under Basil Long until the second World War. A gymnasium was added in 1919, and further building was undertaken in 1921. The school was taken over by G E Hunt, who had established a school at Sharrow in Church Road in 1932 with a few boys, with the help of R J Mowll, through whom a link was forged with Great Walstead in Lindfield.

Brunswick, which claimed to be a preparatory school for Eton and Harrow, was to be found in Oathall Road on the site now occupied by St Paul's school. It was established in the 1890s by the Misses Charlotte and Kate Thompson, but early in the next century it was taken over by Llewellyn C W Thring, a Cambridge graduate

There was another well established boys' school in Bolnore Road, on the western edge of the town. Belvedere was established by Stephen Yeates in the late 1880s, and in 1888 he added an iron schoolroom to the house. He was a Henfield man, and was aged 62 in 1891; at that time his school included 28 boarders aged between 8 and 14, together with a cook, housemaid, kitchen-maid and two young assistant masters. One of these was Charles Julius Dunn Gregory, a Lincolnshire man aged 19 at the time. By 1899 he had succeeded as headmaster. Yeates probably had died; a fishmonger then listed in Sussex Road, William Yeates, may well have been his son. Gregory became a university graduate by 1915, and the school prospered under his guidance, for he extended the school buildings in 1923.

There was, however a girls' school in Oathall Road which still flourishes near Horsham. In March 1896 Edith Buller, who had been teaching in London, moved with her sister Mary from Norton Leas into Farlington House, which had been built for them to the north of Petlands, with the intention of offering a Christian education for 16 girls at most. After little more than two years, however, Edith Buller fell terminally ill, and the sisters were succeeded by two sisters in their twenties, Isobel and Charlotte Moberly, who maintained the religious ambience Edith Buller had initiated. At first the girls attended St Wilfrid's church on Sundays, but after 1900 they went to the chapel of the

Holy Spirit in Sydney Road.

Under the new regime the school prospered; the premises were extended, and Little Farlington next to Middle Farm nearby, which had been built by James Longley of Crawley, was acquired as a junior department. It housed 8 juniors by 1901, and later became a residentiary annexe; by that time there were 27 girls in the senior school. Mrs Moberly and a third sister, Alice, were also involved in the running of the school.

Discipline was always a primary concern, and the academic aspirations of the school were stimulated by Miss Edith Stock between 1900 and 1910; later, specialist teachers of both sexes joined the staff. The school moved to Strood Park, near Warnham, at Christmastide, 1954.

There were other successful girls' schools. One established nearby at this period was at Trevelyan in Church Road. This had been founded at the end of the century by Miss Minnie Rose, who previously had had a school at Holly House in Paddockhall Road. By 1900 Trevelyan had been taken over by the Misses Bull, who had come from Brixton in south London, and was said by the *Mid Sussex Times* to be attracting 'excellent reports'. A gymnasium was added in 1904, and the buildings were extended further by the Misses Rolfe and Kelsey in 1925-6. The school closed in 1966, with 150 girls still on its books. The building was demolished in 1985.

Another was that at Hengistbury in Milton Road. This was run by the daughters of Francis Holloway, who had become an 'architect and surveyor' by the time the school opened about 1881. When the Census was taken on 3 April he had at home with him a son aged 28, described as a carpenter, and four daughters, the three eldest of whom were aged between 20 and 26. Of these the eldest, Lucy Mary, was described as a schoolmistress; the next, Delta Jane, was, perhaps inadvertently, given no occupation, although in the following year she was shown running a 'ladies school' with her sister Lucy; the youngest of the group, Charlotte Catherine, was described as an 'assistant schoolmistress'. The youngest of the sisters was Edith Alice. She was aged only 12 at the time, but in due course she became an Associate of the London College of Music, and was teaching music at Hengistbury before the first World War.

There were also a short-lived establishment for girls at The Berea in Church Road about 1900, and a school in Gordon Road which needed to extend its premises in 1909. Some of these schools seem not to have been run to provide a living for their principals. For a short time before the first World War Dorothy Adams was running a school at Sydney House in Sydney Road, where her mother appeared to be head of the household. Others were well established enterprises that survived for many years. The Misses Messieux ran a more successful school at Oakdene in Paddockhall Road, and Parkfield preparatory school had been established by the Rev Lewis Evans in the 1890s in what was once a private house, now Downlands Park nursing home in Isaacs Lane. This was still flourishing in the mid 1930s.

At first schools were near the centre of the town, close to St Wilfrid's church, but later they came to be concentrated more on the Oathall-Hazelgrove Road area. A number were set up near the railway station, notably at Hengistbury in Milton Road. There was at least one school in Boltro Road shortly before the second World War: St Mary's Hall, a girls' school under the headship of Miss Irene Heaton that accepted also small boys, was in the house now known as Maxwelton. Later this school was moved to Brighton.

A number of private teachers also appeared, mostly briefly, over the years. One was a graduate named A A Ogle, who was active as a private tutor in Hazelgrove Road around 1915. Others offered more specific subjects. Thomas Patching was teaching dancing in South Road in the early 1880s, as was Vera Sutton at Arnolds in Church Road shortly after the first World War. There were also those who taught music. Miss Walker was active in Sydney Road about 1880, and besides Edith Holloway in the early years of this century there were Sophia Wedler and Ruth Towner in Haywards Road.

In 1902 Fraulein Wedler, a diplomee of the Berlin Academy, was to be found at St Katherine's in Little Haywards Road. She mortgaged property in Haywards Road in 1903, and in 1907 was at Parkhurst. She returned to Germany at the outbreak of the first World War while retaining a financial interest in her property. Miss Towner was active in the town during the inter-war period, and for some time was the organist at St Richard's church.

Holy Cross convent, Bolnore Road, now Grosvenor Hall.

The kitchen at Holy Cross convent.

Class of girls at Holy Cross convent.

Class of 1910, St Wilfrid's infants school.

THE TOWN'S CENTRES

E ARLY in the century four centres were identified in the town: Boltro
Road, Commercial Square, South Road and Sussex Road. We turn to look
at these in more detail.

Market Place and Commercial Square

On 3 October 1934 the range of buildings in Market Place standing opposite
the railway line were auctioned. These were owned by Charles Golding and
Sons. At the beginning of the century they had erected a coachhouse, stables a
pair of shops and some houses, together with a bank. On the north was Arthur
Bridges' well established bootmaker's workshop, in front of four old cottages
let to men probably employed by Golding's, F Botting, C Cook, C H Peake
and H Simmons respectively. The cattle market stood on the west and south of
these buildings. Caffyn's garage was built here in 1935, when the company
also built a workshop in Church Road and cottages, presumably for staff quarters,
in Queens Road. A road across Harlands farm was proposed in April 1934,
and Harlands fields were designated in 1938 for an extension of the market
site; but Harlands Road seems not to have appeared for another 25 years.

To the north stood the offices of Thomas Bannister by the railway bridge.
The market extended northwards behind Bannister's office complex. The site
also had other uses. In 1910 there was a drill hall, which was still in use during
the second World War. This may have been the premises proposed for a rifle
club in 1905. In 1914 Philip Perry erected a temporary theatre in 'Bannister's
field'.

Beyond that was the Station Hotel. This stood back from the road, and was
the principal lot in the sale. There were ten bedrooms for guests, four for staff
and a billiard room. A room on the south side was used by traders on market
days, and for social and other functions. In later years the hotel was called The
Hayworthe or The Hayworthe Arms.

The remaining buildings appeared much as they do today. On a site formerly
occupied by the grocer's and butcher's shops next to the hotel stood Bank
Buildings. As now, the facade of the building was in two distinct sections, the
first having one gable and the second two. Barclays Bank occupied the first of
these sections and a half of the second; the bank extended its premises in 1920

from those it first leased about 1907 as its first branch in the town to replace the agency run by the solicitor Edward Waugh. At that time Parkhurst and Company, a firm of furniture dealers, and Stephen Pierce and Sons, butchers, were to be found in Market Place, probably on the same site. The fourth section of the building was leased and occupied by George Hilton and Sons in 1934; from 1920 these premises had been occupied by C G Prevett Ltd, a firm of general engineers.

Golding's motor works dated from 1913. They consisted of a garage and filling station which at one time housed taxis, with three petrol pumps standing on the pavement in front, and a motor workshop with lockup garages behind. They became Brown's garage when Fred Fairhall transferred the business from South Road to join Chris Jones in 1979.

Boltro Chambers also date from earlier years. In 1907 a solicitor, Lawrence Wyatt, was to be found there, and a dentist, Charles Witcombe, was listed in *Kelly's directory* as holding a surgery there on two days a week in 1915. The estate agents Bradley and Vaughan, formed when Hedley Vaughan joined E Bradley in 1909, were based there also before they moved to St Clair Lodge in 1932. Another firm of estate agents, Scott Pitcher, was to be found opposite at the bottom of Boltro Road, conveniently near both the station and the hotel. In 1934 the building housed two suites of offices, both leased to Charles W Whitcombe, very possibly the dentist who had practised there and perhaps the Charles Whitcomb living at 62 Richmond Road, Worthing; a firm of solicitors, Stevens, Son and Pope, and an architect, Harold Turner occupied the chambers in 1938. A plot of land lay beyond, opposite the police station. This seems to have remained unoccupied until the telephone exchange was built about 1965.

In 1989 Haywards Heath Market plc, who owned the market once run by Thomas Bannister, ceased to hold the Sunday stall market which the District Council had allowed in November 1983. The market site was sold to Sainsbury's, who had opened a branch in South Road the day following the Golding's auction. Bannister's offices were demolished, together with the pair of old cottages they incorporated and the other market buildings; these included the old drill hall, then serving as the market canteen. Bannister Way was built to provide a link road from Harlands Road to the new supermarket. This was opened on 10 September 1991.

South Road and Sussex Square

At the turn of the century commercial activity in South Road was polarized. At The Broadway opposite the church schools (now occupied by Christian Scientists) stood Stanford Place. A butcher named Arthur Alwen occupied

99

Number 6. A terrace of four private houses known as Stanford Terrace (or Stanford Place) came next, followed by John Edward Piper's general stores at Stanford House. This included the Muster Green post office that replaced Muster House, and was continued as Cobb's stores, which incorporated the adjoining shop as a draper's shop. Mr Piper had come from Cuckfield to South Road, where he had traded for twenty years. In 1908 he sought to move to The Broadway, but evidently his business did not prosper, and he had ceased to trade about 1914.

Beyond stood Victoria Park, where a fire station was built in 1903, and St Hilda's Cottages and Edelweiss, where Alfred Willmot ran his own school. At the junction with Haywards Road stood Heather Cottages, a pair of houses owned by Mrs Harmes, the teacher in charge of the infants' school, who lived in one with her husband John, an insurance agent.

On the opposite side of South Road was open land, part of which was used to extend the churchyard, next to two large houses, Heathmere, which stood opposite Haywards Road, and Brent Eleigh, to which stables were added in 1903, and which became the house of Dr Frederick Robson. Both houses were demolished to make way for commercial development, Heathmere in 1935 and Brent Eleigh in 1980, when the Orchards shopping precinct was built.

Heather Cottages stood opposite Canton Cottage across the top of Haywards Road. The latter cottage was at the end of a row of three pairs of semi-detached houses, of which the gables of one pair, Laurel Cottages, may still be seen. Beyond them stood a block of three shops, two of which were occupied by tradesmen named Watts: Charles, a bootmaker and repairer, and George Albert, a greengrocer who had set up in business in 1881. George was in Laurel Cottages in 1899. Charles had mortgaged the cottages in 1897 for £300, but sold one of them to George shortly afterwards. Charles disappeared early in the next century.

George was still active in 1924, when other members of the family also were trading in the road. In 1920 Mrs Ellen Watts agreed to allow a right of way between the east side of her shop and the 'property' of Mrs Maria June Watts next door. Maria was trading as a greengrocer near the Congregational church, and a Mrs E Watts was trading as a greengocer as late as 1938.

Next came a pair of houses occupied as a grocery and a private residence by William Henry Raven, who had succeeded a Mr Carr. On the opposite side of the road stood the premises taken over by George Hilton in 1888, next to the grounds around Heathmere, and beside them was a block of cottages called Pelham Terrace or Pelham Place.

Further towards Sussex Square on the right there were three pairs of semi-detached houses. The first house served as both residence and office for the manager of the water works, and Lyntonville served a similar dual function for the Plummer family in Hazelgrove Road. The third pair, Cedar Villas, also served as business premises; the first housed a dentist's surgery and a solicitor's office, and in the second Edward Parrott, a cab proprietor, was to be found, with stables at the rear. Next came the public hall, with the Constitutional Club and the hall of the Church Lads Brigade behind in Gower Road. On the opposite side of the road was the shop of E Grimsdick and Son, nurserymen, whose garden reached the cross-roads.

Towards Crossways (Sussex Square) were three pairs of shops. The first pair consisted of a milliner's, Regent House, run by Mrs M A Uridge, the wife of the grocer Henry Uridge, and the greengrocer's of Eliel Walder, who was also to be found in Mill Green Road. The next pair were occupied by Alfred Maller, an ironmonger and plumber, whose shop was taken over by Mr Walder in 1901, and by Henry Uridge, trading as Uridge and Son, grocers and drapers, Crossways Stores. The third pair, on the corner of Sussex Road, comprised the shops of Cephas Chandler, a butcher, and George Fenner, a draper. By 1924 Freeman, Hardy and Willis, shoe retailers, had followed him.

By 1907 Mr Chandler had been replaced by a bootmaker, John Field, who also had a shop in Queens Road. Soon the fishmonger Percy Rowland came into the premises previously occupied by Mrs Uridge, Henry's wife, next to the public hall. He added stabling to his shop, and was enterprising enough to speculate in property as far away as Brighton. By 1928 the Home and Colonial Stores came to occupy the old premises of Rice Brothers, then trading as saddlers, at Number 26, on the site occupied by Budgen's superstore since 1992. The International Tea Stores had arrived before 1924, and extended the shop they occupied in 1930.

Two enterprises from the earliest days survived into the 1980s: George Hilton's business and Grimsdick's nursery were established in the early 1880s. The firm of Muzzell and Hilton, later Hilton and Clarke and finally Horace Hilton, dated from the 1920s, and the grocer Frank Brenchley had established himself at Number 105 by 1926, and by 1967 the business was being run by his son Gordon Brenchley. Barclays Bank opened a branch on 12 April 1928, and by 1938 another branch had appeared on the opposite side of the road; this was still operative in 1950. Other prominent traders survived from the 1920s until recent years; by 1926 the outfitters Haines and Sharp had arrived in Pelham Place.

The road underwent extensive building development during the 1930s; the garden of Brent Eleigh disappeared as early as 1934. In 1934 Lloyds Bank planned to open a sub-branch on the corner of Haywards Road, and Boots opened a branch at Number 108. In April 1935 12 shops opposite Victoria

Park with accommodation over were planned, and eight shops with flats were proposed for the corner of Haywards Road in 1937. The chemists Timothy Whites and Taylors, the fruiterers and greengrocers T Walton and the circulating library of Quinton Edwards Ltd (known as 'the Q library') were to be found in South Road by 1938, as were the optician G C Bateman and Woolworth's, who had a store in South Parade.

On 4 October 1934 Sainsbury's opened their first branch in the town at 110 South Road. This was at 3 South Parade, in a parade of shops that can still be identified by a brick bearing the letters 'JBS' (the initials of the then chairman of the company) beside a path leading to The Orchards shopping precinct that crosses the site of the garden at Brent Eleigh. Cheyne Investments Ltd, a subsidiary of Sainsbury's, built the block of shops to secure the central position for Sainsbury's, letting the remaining shop sites to retailers with a range of goods and services that would attract trade in the area.

Substantial business development has taken place in the post-war period. In 1971 Sainsbury's store was moved across the road to 29 South Road, a site beside the public hall that eventually it absorbed; the premises are now occupied by Budgen's. In 1981 Boots shop was to move to larger premises at the end of the block which later were taken over by Timothy Whites and in 1984 by Curry's. More spectacular is The Orchards shopping precinct built by W C Hilton over the site of George Hilton's store and financed by Norwich Union. This was opened on 12 October 1982 as Priory Walk, and in 1985 sculptures were added at the Church Road end. The adjacent store was originally one of Gateway's superstores, but it was replaced by a Marks and Spencer store in 1991.

Sussex Road

Sussex Road is a short section of a well-established thoroughfare leading from Newchapel on the Surrey border on the north to Ditchling and Brighton on the south. The road became a turnpike in 1770. The area bounded by the Sussex Hotel, Triangle Road and Franklynn Road formed a distinct group including cottages on the north side of South Road near Crossways, and was known in 1871 as The Triangle.

It was an area peopled by small shopkeepers and craftsmen, and included a few elderly people. Living conditions must often have been cramped, but a number of the households included lodgers living independently, one of whom is described as a 'schoolmaster (dissenting)'. In 1874 the west side of the road was still undeveloped; there were only a pair of semi-detached houses called 'Grove Cottages' and a brickfield opposite Triangle Place.

In 1894 the Haywards Heath and District Industrial Co-operative Society was established near the junction with Gower Road. It merged with the East Grinstead society in 1911 and with the Brighton society in 1924, and became very active in that part of the town, where its philosophy had a particular appeal. In the early years of this century its facilities were considerably extended. The branch closed in 1987, and the present building is now divided into a number of smaller businesses.

In May 1902 Horace Walter Selby set up in business as a chemist at no 18, next door to the shop that still bears his name; the original shop still has traces of his mural advertisement. At first he lived with his family over the shop. He had been told by the Grimsdick family in Hazelgrove Road that there was a need for a chemist in that part of the town, and he came from Nottingham to complement the only other chemist in the Broadway. He moved to a shop at the corner of Sussex Square in 1913, and extended his premises in 1930. His was one of a number of retail pharmacies in Mid Sussex acquired by Mr V E Seanor about 1939 which were named after him.

There was also an art needlework shop at Number 20 run by Mabel Scutt. She was the youngest child of a confectioner named Henry Scutt, at 26 and 28 in 1915, and his wife Louisa. A similar situation seems to have arisen in connection with the grocer's business of Thomas Francis Green. He was listed as being in business by 1924; but by 1932 the business had been taken over by his wife Edith, although he was still alive.

In 1924 twenty-three tradespeople were listed in *Kelly's directory*. In addition to a number of butchers and grocers, they included an upholsterer, fancy draper, fried fish shop and, strangely enough, a car hire firm. There were two bakers: Edward Cole and Son at Number 13 had been in business there since 1899, and William Crees at Number 40 had come from Maresfield. Sarah Johnson was in business as a builder at Number 38. Charles Knight at Number 26 described himself as a confectioner in 1924, but by 1938 he had become an 'oil and colour man'. On the other hand, Thomas Luck was living at 1 Grove Cottages (Number 34) between 1915 and 1938, and was a watch repairer in his spare time. His daughter Nellie was still living there in 1967 with her sister Annie.

In recent years the pattern of businesses in the road has changed radically. The name Selby is still associated with a chemist's business, and the Heath Hotel is the old Triangle. Otherwise all has changed.

Boltro Chambers, Market Place, in 1934. On the right
is Golding's (now Brown's) garage.

Barclays Bank (now Barclay Court), Market Place, 1934.

The Station Hotel, Market Place, in 1934. Now Zenith House.

View past the cattle market. In the foreground is the
boundary hedge of Bannister's offices.

Bannister's offices (now demolished). Caffyn's garage is to the left of the picture. The original pair of cottages are on the right.

Last days of the cattle market. View of the market from the entrance. The offices are on the left.

The market canteen. This was the former drill hall, which was commandeered for military purposes in 1939-45.

The pens for cattle. Burrell Road is in the background.

Commercial Square *c*1900.

The present Sainsbury's superstore on the old market site.

Above, The Sussex
Hotel *c*1900.

Right, J W Dinnage's first
shop, opposite the Heath
Hotel in Sussex Road. The
figure on the left is
probably Mr Dinnage.

THE LAST FIFTY YEARS

HAYWARDS Heath sustained little damage during the second World War. In 1940 a bomb fell on houses between Haywards Road and Wood Ride, and inflicted some damage on South Road; another damaged the cricket pavilion in Clair Meadow and Perrymount Road.

In 1943 the Haywards Heath County secondary school (now Oathall Community College) commenced an agricultural course as a school farm which was integrated into the school curriculum, and this supplied the school canteen. Its students attended Plumpton Agricultural College for the first five years, before the course was moved to Beckworth House in Lindfield.

The telephone exchange was housed in the post office building next to the magistrates' court in Boltro Road, before 1963, when the present exchange was built next to Boltro Chambers opposite the former police station in Paddockhall Road, and subscriber trunk dialling was introduced. Hengistbury, which was standing derelict nearby, was demolished finally in 1975.

The local population had increased markedly as a result of the war. In 1939 the Urban District contained 13,880 residents. During hostilities the figure fluctuated, presumably because of varying numbers of evacuees, but in 1946 there were still 14,820 people resident in the district. During the 1950s an increasing number of workers commuted to London, and the population rose from about 17,000 to 18,460. In 1981 the district contained 28,465 people, but by 1991 there were only 22,000 residents.

The demand for residential accommodation and leisure facilities was increasing in the south east, and businesses were invading the region. The earlier character of the town was gradually transformed. The town still possessed its own prize band in 1951, and in the summer of that year an Overseas Club was opened for foreigners in the area.

Many houses experienced a change of use, a common urban phenomenon. Others made way for more radical developments. In the 1950s and 1960s large houses such as Winnals in Paddockhall Road, Winkfield in Boltro Road near-by and Jireh and Ormerod in Perrymount Road made way for denser development as flats, although some larger houses such as East Franklands in Lewes Road, Chandos Lodge in Paddockhall Road and others on Muster Green have remained. To the south of Muster Green Oakwood made way for sheltered housing built by the Sussex Housing Association for the Aged, although the

District Council had opposed residential development on the adjacent Great Haywards farm.

In the early 1960s Oakfield in Perrymount Road was rebuilt as offices, and about the same time three office blocks were built on open land adjacent to the market site (now Bannister Way) in Harlands Road, and the industrial estates in Burrell Road and Bridge Road were constructed. The creeping commercialization of the area caused the closure in 1984 of the Hayworthe Arms hotel, as the Station Hotel came to be known, and its conversion into another office building, known as Hayworthe House and later Zenith House, between Radnor House and the former Barclays Bank offices.

In 1991-2 Heath Square in Boltro Road was built on the site of the former offices of the Rural District Council, and office development was continued towards Market Place about 1995 with the demolition of the post office to make way for the present Job Centre.

These and other developments generated an increase in the volume of traffic caused the construction of two gyratory road systems, one at Star Corner at The Broadway about 1968 and the other, converting Milton Road from a cul-de-sac into a through road to Harlands Road, in the early 1970s. The bulk of the Harlands Farm estate had been sold by 1958.

The residential development of the estate and population growth in the area, with the consequent increase in the number of children of school age, led to the establishment of the grammar school in 1958. Harlands primary school in Penland Road was opened on 10 February 1965. The secondary school had been one of the first to enter pupils for the General Certificate of Education in 1951, when St Wilfrid's school was moved to Eastern Road. Mr D W S Jarvis transferred from Haywards Heath County secondary modern school to join the new grammar school as its head. The grammar school became comprehensive, catering for youngsters aged 11-18, about 1974, and a sixth form college in April 1993 under the Further Education Funding Council. It became a further education college by 1996.

A county branch library was opened in the early 1960s on land belonging to the Urban District Council in Boltro Road. In 1967 an Evangelical Free church was built in New England Road, and the Church of the Good Shepherd was built in Franklands Village about this time. A short-lived project sponsored by the churches that aimed to cater for the leisure interests of young people was The Carnaby Pew coffee bar in South Road. This was started in March 1968, and was open on Wednesdays, Fridays and Saturdays; but the enterprise closed down in response to complaints from local residents of rowdiness late at night.

The District Council's Dolphin leisure centre in Pasture Hill Road was first opened in May 1976, when it included the swimming pools, squash courts and sauna facility. It was visited by Princess Alexandra on 13 June 1977, and its resources were extended in 1991. Occasionally it serves as an alternative venue to Clair Hall, which had been opened in 1974, as a theatre and concert hall. The privately run Platform Theatre, established in a disused warehouse in Burrell Road in September 1992, was forced to close in July 1996.

In 1987 the Town Council was constituted from the former Neighbourhood Council, which had existed for two years. The Town Hall in Boltro Road was opened in October 1990 at a cost of £279,000. A fresh magistrates' court and sub-divisional police headquarters were built between 1990 and 1992 on the site of Elfinsward at the junction of Bolnore Road with Muster Green; the police authority had acquired the site in 1973, and in 1993 a technologically advanced new hospital, the Princess Royal, was opened on land at the other end of the town adjacent to the old St Francis hospital, which was closed in November 1995. It replaces the Cuckfield and Haywards Heath hospitals.

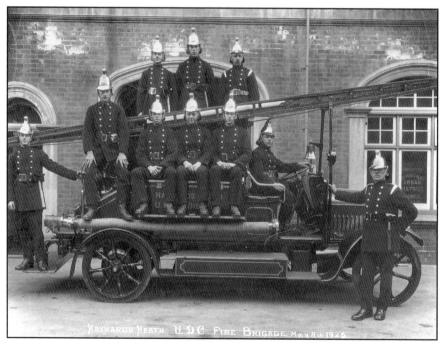

Haywards Heath Urban District Fire Brigade outside the UDC offices in Boltro Road, photographed on May 8, 1926, by George Banbury of South Road.

THE PRESENT SCENE

IN the post-War period residential housing has increased dramatically in response to a rapid increase in population, particularly to the west of Paddockhall Road and east of Hazelgrove Road. Traces of the earlier history of the town may be seen in its forty-eight listed buildings, and some of the old names have been preserved to remind us of the early rural landscape.

Franklands Village is on the site of Franklands Wood and Franklands farm, Penland Road preserves the name of a farm, and Northlands Wood survives as an area of residential housing. The Priory estate has been developed from the land of the former religious community which moved to Sayers Common. Barnmead recalls the bungalow that once stood on the Bridgers mill land west of Balcombe Road, where once Caleb Higgs lived.

Leisure facilities, however, have not kept pace with this expansion, although Blunts and Paiges Woods between Haywards Heath and Cuckfield are now public nature reserves, and a smaller reserve exists near Scrase Bridge. Muster Green was designated a conservation area in 1979.

Commercial activity in the town is now increasingly dominated by large enterprises. Many of the former private dwellings have become offices, and the much of the west side of Perrymount Road now houses various branches of Lloyds Bank. The east side of Boltro Road now consists of professional and business offices. In December 1971 the Royal Commonwealth Society for the Blind opened its offices beside the Midland Bank at the corner of Heath Road; later the Society, now known as Sightsavers, moved to Grosvenor Hall, the site of the former convent in Bolnore Road.

Long established local enterprises have also suffered from absorption by larger organizations. The trend was evident much earlier in the ownership by breweries of public houses: Nalder and Collyer once owned the Liverpool Arms, and by the late 1920s The Star was owned by Portsmouth United Breweries, the Burrell Arms by Tamplins, and the Sergison Arms by Page and Overton in the early 1930s. The Birch Hotel remained independent well into the post-War period. The business founded by the builder W C Hilton in 1926 was incorporated in 1967. The *Mid Sussex Times* is now owned by a newspaper conglomerate, and the dairy set up in Cuckfield by Jack Gubbin before the War became J Gubbin and Sons, with a depot in Burrell Road, and was taken over by Unigate Dairies in 1995, who quit the site in the following January.

Haywards Heath Building Society was merged with the Yorkshire Building Society in January 1993, but estate agents and other building societies have continued to flourish, and developers of residential property exploit the potential of the area.

There is also commercial development by large organizations: The Orchards shopping precinct in South Road was financed by Norwich Union. But perhaps the development that has had the greatest effect on the town's economy has been the establishment of the Sainsbury's superstore near the station, close to the site once occupied by Beeny's stores.

The railway still caters for those who commute daily to their places of work, and increasingly spaces are needed for the cars of those who work in the town in addition to those who use the railway. In May 1996 the Mid Sussex District Council issued a draft development brief for the land on the east of the railway track and south of the station, one of the last large sites in the town remaining to be developed. The closure of the Liverpool Arms beside the track in 1991, and its demolition in the summer of 1997 on the ground that it was dilapidated, removed yet another landmark in the history of the town, and hinted at what may come in the future. The old intimacy has gone, to be replaced by a more impersonal atmosphere; and the town may now be seen indeed as 'the metropolis of Mid Sussex'.

BIBLIOGRAPHY

UNPUBLISHED

Church Commissioners, files 23227, 28510
Public Record Office, Census returns, 1841-91 (HO; RG9/582, RG10/1061, RG11/1062, RG12/792)
Sussex Archaeological Society, deeds series D,DD,WA
West Sussex Record Office, Brookeborough (Sergison) papers; Cuckfield tithe award (1843); minutes of Cuckfield vestry meetings; map of manors of Heyworth and Trubwick (1638) and records of the manorial court (1805-1905); enclosure awards for Haywards Heath and Wivelsfield (1861-2)
Haywards Heath Urban District Council. Registers of planning applications, 1878-1950

PRINTED

Barker, Eric, 'Sussex Anglo-Saxon charters', Sussex Archaeological Collections (SAC), 86, pp 47-101; 87, pp 112-63; 88, pp 51-114
Clarke's local directory and year book for Cuckfield, Haywards Heath, Lindfield and Burgess Hill. Haywards Heath, C Clarke, [1879]
Cooper, JH 'Cuckfield families: the Wardens', SAC 49, pp 89-104
Cooper, MH 'A perambulation of Cuckfield', SAC 61, pp 40-62
Ford, Wyn K 'Boltro farm, Cuckfield', SAC 114, pp 81-96
   'William Allen and the Lindfield agricultural colony', Sussex History 22, pp 24-36
   The story of the Haywards Heath Building Society, 1890—1990. The Society, [1990]
   'The first forty years. Early mortgages and mortgagors of the Haywards Heath Building Society', SAC 130, pp 213-31
   The church in Sussex Road. Haywards Heath Methodist church, 1994
Garrett, Elizabeth. Farlington School, 1896-1996: a centenary history. Privately printed, [1995]
Haywards Heath County Secondary School. Sure foundations, [by A.G. Maller]. C Clarke, [1959]
Kelly's directory for Sussex, 1845-1938
Mid-Sussex directory and visitors' guide for 1967. C Clarke
Mid Sussex Times
Minutes of evidence taken before the House of Lords committee ... London and Brighton railway via Shoreham (HL 1836, vol 34(i)) (Copy in Brighton area reference library)
Renshaw, WC 'The hundred of Buttinghill', SAC 58, pp 6-20
Sussex Record Society series
   vol. 7. An abstract of feet of fines ... II, ed LF Salzman. 1907
   vol.10. The three earliest subsidies ... ed W Hudson. 1910
   vol 13. The parish registers of Cuckfield, ed WC Renshaw. 1911
   vol 19. Sussex manors ... recorded in the feet of fines, ed EHW Dunkin. 1914
   vol 29. Abstracts of Sussex deeds ... ed W Budgen. 1924
   vol 33. Sussex inquisitions ... ed MS Holgate. 1927
   vol 34. The book of John Rowe ... 1597-1622, ed WH Godfrey. 1928
   vol 44. Records of the barony and honour of ... Lewes, ed AJ Taylor. 1944
Wyatt, TG Fifty years of church work in ... Haywards Heath, 1856-1906. 1906 (Distributed with the parish magazine for June, 1906)
   Twelve years of church work ... 1906-1918. 1918

INDEX

References to illustrations are included. Names of houses are generally excluded, as are names of places outside the neighbouring area.

118

119

120